The Zero-Mile *Diet*
COOKBOOK

The ZERO-MILE *Diet* COOKBOOK

Seasonal Recipes for Delicious Homegrown Food

Carolyn Herriot

Harbour Publishing

This page: Corn and Bean Salsa (recipe, page 153)

*Previous page, clockwise from lower left: Zero-Mile summer picnic—Fresh Mint Tabouleh
(page 159); Mediterranean Stuffed Grape Leaves (page 171); Potato, Mint and Pea Salad (page
156); Cinco de Mayo Slaw (page 157); Raspberry Lemon Verbena Iced Tea (page 186); Berry
Yummy Sponge Cake (page 181).*

CONTENTS

About the Symbols

These symbols help identify recipes suitable to your (or your guest's) dietary preferences:

GF = Gluten-free   **VG** = Vegan

* = Gluten-free or vegan with modification

Ingredients this colour are those you can grow yourself (Or purchase from a local farmer)

PREFACE

Spending time with Carolyn Herriot at her cozy home while working with her on *The Zero-Mile Diet Cookbook: Seasonal Recipes for Delicious Homegrown Food*—sister book to her bestselling *The Zero-Mile Diet: A Year-Round Guide to Growing Organic Food*—was deeply inspiring and, unquestionably, delicious.

Centred on simple yet superb plant-based meals that reflect the season, Carolyn routinely serves up such treats as homemade Pasta with Camille's Nettle Pesto, Zucchini Ribbons with Rice, Three Sisters Soup, Beet Hummus, Mediterranean Stuffed Grape Leaves, Goldie's Quince and Sunchoke Roast, Creamy Parsnip and Apple Soup and Crispy Kale Chips. Meals are crowned with such garden delicacies as Herbal Espresso, Lavender Macaroons, Rhubarb Strawberry Galettes and orchard-inspired liqueurs and berry cordial. Dried fruit and vegetables, and jars of Green Tomato Relish, Rhubarb Ginger Chutney, antipasto, salsas, jams and jellies, as well as pickled beans, garlic, asparagus and crabapples, line her larder.

Just outside Carolyn's kitchen, her garden beckons. The arbour-covered "berry walk" leads past herbs, kale, crinkly cress, magenta sprean, 'Tres Fine Marche' endive and 'Dragon Tongue' beans, and then down to the orchard of apples, pears, peaches and plums. A cheery cluster of copper-feathered chickens, who recycle garden parings into giant eggs, cluck-cluck amidst the satisfying thrum of honeybees in the recently adopted hive. The greenhouse bursts with potted 'Pepperoncini' and 'Tequila Sunrise' peppers, purple tomatillos and 'Flamme' and 'Graham's Goodkeeper' tomatoes, among other heirlooms. Red amaranth and multi-hued quinoa bow under their loads of seeds. At every step, organic bounty abounds, bursting with flavour and ready for picking.

Living a zero-mile lifestyle has a lovely rhythm that connects us deeply with the flow of the seasons and earth that surrounds us. Using simple strategies for growing food and her own collection of garden-to-kitchen recipes developed over two decades, Carolyn easily fills the pantry with organic homegrown goodies to take a household right through the year.

Whether we grow our own or support local farmers, this is the book to rely on for in-season sustainable cooking inspiration. With a culinary-herb A-Z and tips on gardening with edibles, *The Zero-Mile Diet Cookbook* contains 160 plant-based recipes with over 100 vegan options and 100 gluten-free dishes, including probiotic foods and recipes for preserving the harvest—in which the seasonal ingredients that Carolyn grows and gathers herself are highlighted. And this is the food that you can grow too.

Honouring health and sustainability, *The Zero-Mile Diet Cookbook* helps us live well and eat ethically. This is the book that tells us what we really need in our kitchens for a no-waste workspace. This is the book that connects us directly to what we are harvesting in our backyard or buying at the local farm market. This is the book that supports us in feeding our kids well and teaching them what is "real" food. And this is the book I will be giving to my children to help them decide how to live and eat as they step out into our world.

Carol Pope
Garden editor

GRATITUDE

As I near the completion of this, my third book, I cannot help but be filled with gratitude. My first book, *A Year on the Garden Path: A 52-Week Organic Gardening Guide*, was an "experiment" to see if I could write—and if people would read it. It worked! I moved onto my second book feeling more confident, and happily many people also expressed gratitude for *The Zero-Mile Diet: A Year-Round Guide to Growing Organic Food*. I am so grateful that my editors convinced me to write a sequel, because I had no idea how very much this book would teach me.

I live a life for which I have every reason to be grateful. Every day I wake up in the peaceful part of the world where I live. I am in good health with lots of energy. I have plenty of everything I need. I have never known deep hunger, felt real danger or lived in absolute poverty. I share my life with a loving husband who enriches it, and many other wonderful people who are kind and caring. I LOVE my life and I am so grateful to be able to say this.

Throughout my life, I have been supported by many incredible people who have helped me to grow the garden of my dreams. If you are one of those people, or have ever been, then know that I am deeply grateful for you and the way you touched my life.

I am particularly grateful to Goldenrose Paquette, the most perfect person to share the kitchen with while I wrote a cookbook. Her ideas and perspective

Carolyn Herriot at home with Guy Dauncey.

enabled me to combine the wisdom I have gained since the 1970s with the wisdom of a young woman firmly rooted in the twenty-first century. Thank you, Goldie, for bridging this gap for me!

I am (surprisingly) grateful to be alive during a time when we are at a crossroads where we hold our survival in our hands. Fortunately, I sleep well every night in the belief that we do care enough about saving ourselves to change the way we live—and for this I am the most grateful.

"At critical points in evolution all living systems respond with transcendence and creativity."
—Elisabet Sahtouris, evolutionary biologist and futurist

FOREWORD

When I was a child, my father often called me "the chief cook and bottlewasher," because I stepped into the kitchen when my mother stepped out to get a "real" job! After World War II, women didn't want to go back to the kitchen sink. They'd enjoyed a taste of independence during the war years, and they were desperate to untie their apron strings and explore their potential beyond motherhood and domestic servitude. Who can blame them?

As a result, TV dinners and instant mashed potatoes became a big hit in the 1960s—but these were just not acceptable options for a lover of good food. So I taught myself to cook, using the wonderful palette of ingredients from the local greengrocer, where I worked on Saturdays. (Back then, greengrocers got all their fruits and vegetables from local farmers.)

Eventually I left home to study for a B.Sc. in Food Science at the University of London. Food science—processing, packaging and additives—has come a long way since the 1970s. Who could have imagined then that scientists would lead us down the road to genetically engineered "Frankenfood"?

No one could have imagined that corporations would not safeguard the nutritional quality of the food they produced, leading us to having to make a critical choice today. Will we return to smaller-scale, organic regional food production that feeds and protects the soil, which in turn grows nutritious food that feeds us? Or will we support the continued expansion of agribusiness, a system that produces nutrient-compromised food from degraded soils, now thought to be creating havoc with human health? Today's statistics for cancer, heart disease, diabetes, dementia and other degenerative diseases are causing concern for the quality of life into old age and the sustainability of healthcare systems everywhere.

My personal goal is to reach my "golden years" strong in body, mind and spirit—and my belief is that how I feed myself is what will get me there. We seem to be living in blissful ignorance of the vital role human nutrition plays in maintaining the body's primary functions in good working order. How could it be that while we send spaceships to Mars we don't know how to feed ourselves down here on Earth?

Shouldn't we all know the 51 essential nutrients we need from our food every day? Isn't it worrying that so many people have lost the skill of growing their own food and that the health of local farming is on its knees? Shouldn't we be concerned that food is travelling around the world to reach our dinner tables, food that is grown using an array of high-tech products that remove the soil and sun from the cycle?

I say yes to all these questions. Something that I can do in response is to grow as much of my own food as possible. After just five years of edible landscaping, I was so inspired by our "Garden of Eating" that I wrote a book about it to share my productive food garden with others. Then I realized that a healthy diet does not stop with growing the food, but continues with how you eat the food once it has been harvested and brought from the garden into the kitchen.

The Zero-Mile Diet Cookbook: Seasonal Recipes for Delicious Homegrown Food is a logical companion to my last book, *The Zero-Mile Diet: A Year-Round Guide to Growing Organic Food*. This cookbook is presented by season, so you need only go to the current season to discover simple yet scrummy ways to prepare the vibrant vegetables, flavourful herbs and fabulous fruits growing in your garden or available from the farm market closest to you.

In addition to what to grow, *The Zero-Mile Diet Cookbook* includes chapters on equipping the kitchen in the most efficient and ecological manner, and stocking the pantry so that you will always be in good shape to spontaneously whip up delicious dinners from your own garden. And, in particular, you'll find a comprehensive chapter on food preservation, because that is how you can sustain year-round zero-mile nourishment from a seasonal harvest.

I hope this book will become a favourite in your kitchen and that it will inspire you to take care of your precious self.

Here's to the good life!

Carolyn

THE ZERO-MILE DIET

RECIPES

ON BECOMING A VEGETARIAN

One of the most life-changing decisions I ever made was to fly from London to Vancouver in 1975 to explore the West Coast of Canada. It was love at first sight, and I knew almost immediately that this place was where I wanted to spend the rest of my life. After six months, this "dolly bird" from London found herself sharing a co-operative house with five others who were all vegetarian. The deal was that we each took turns making dinner, and, as I loved cooking, instead of being daunted I dashed out to buy a good vegetarian cookbook. There was no going back for me, and I have been a healthy vegetarian ever since.

It was there at 23 Dunbar Street that I dropped 30 pounds, felt my energy lighten with a greater sense of well-being and realized how important it is to nourish and care for the body. After swallowing John Robbins's *Diet for a New America*, I was clear that I did not want the suffering and inhumanity of concentrated animal feedlot operations (CAFOs) to become part of me.

From conversations at dinner parties, I understand that people are still anxious about getting enough protein from a vegetarian diet, but I assure you this is not a problem. Yes, adequate protein is important for tissue growth and repair, metabolic functioning and disease-fighting antibody formation—but grains, beans, nuts, seeds and dairy products are valuable sources of essential amino acids, and when combined they ensure an adequate intake of protein. One of these three groups of complementary proteins (with fresh vegetables from the garden) will more than satisfy your requirements:

1. Grains combined with beans
2. Grains combined with dairy products
3. Beans combined with seeds

And more limited protein complementarity exists between:

4. Grains combined with seeds
5. Beans combined with dairy products
6. Seeds combined with dairy products

The Thing about Meat

As the planet's population hits seven billion people, we need to consider the implications of making meat the centre of the meal. I find it hard to stomach that we grow corn, beans and grains to feed livestock animals when 870 million people are going hungry, according to the latest UN report. Consider how easily we could feed the world if members of the affluent meat-eating society cut back to eating meat once a week. Just imagine how much suffering to animals we would alleviate if we banned concentrated animal feedlot operations.

This is why the recipes in this book do not contain meat or poultry, even though I have nothing against eating animals if they are raised and allowed to express their natural or essential being—"the essence of piggyness" as pioneering farmer Joel Salatin calls it. However, you will find three recipes for wild salmon, because I am fortunate enough to have a friend with a boat who takes me fishing!

THE GROWING LIST

My refrigerator.

When it comes to good health, I live on the preventative rather than the curative side, which means I take responsibility for my own well-being. I want to know that the food I eat is nourishing my body, and I believe that the fruits and vegetables best for me are those grown in nutrient-rich soil and ripened under the sun. Therefore, my best reassurance comes from growing as much of my own food as possible and, after that, supporting local organic farmers' stands.

There's something grounding about growing your own food, and in uncertain times it's reassuring to know you will always find something good to eat and feed to your family in your own backyard or community garden. My zero-mile diet means that I regularly eat food grown lovingly and harvested from the garden shortly before the meal is eaten. Surely there can be nothing better for me than that?

As this cookbook has been written as a companion book to *The Zero-Mile Diet: A Year-Round Guide*

to Growing Organic Food, many of the recipes are peppered with photos from my garden and with growing tips, but for in-depth information on growing your own vegetables, fruits and herbs (as well as saving seeds), I recommend you refer to my first book.

In addition, in the hundred or so recipes included in this book, I have taken the step of highlighting ingredients you can grow yourself. But if you do not have these edibles in your garden yet, don't panic. Your local farm market will likely be an excellent source, and in the meantime, the highlighted ingredients are simply meant as food for thought on what you might like to grow yourself one day, and what is most likely to be grown locally if you are reading this book in a temperate climate.

To save paper and ink in the recipe sections "organic" does not precede every ingredient, but I do recommend you seek out organic products such as organic flour, dairy products and produce when it is not possible to grow or make your own. It's worth it!

Here is a comprehensive A to Z of all the edible plants you'll find growing information on in *The Zero-Mile Diet: A Year-Round Guide to Growing Organic Food*, or in the added tips in this book. These plants (as well as local honey, eggs from backyard hens and foraged wild ingredients like nettles and seaweed) form the basis of the recipes in this cookbook, and even though this list may seem extensive, all of the plants can be grown in an average suburban setting with adequate exposure to sunlight. If you haven't grown any of these edibles before, I encourage you to make a start by edible landscaping your yard, signing up for a community garden or adding some salad pots to your patios—and then to think about expanding your own growing list for a zero-mile diet.

Amaranth • Anise • Apple • Apricot • Artichoke • Arugula • Asian Pear • Asparagus • Basil • Bay • Beans • Beet • Blackberry • Blueberry • Borage • Broad Bean (Fava) • Broccoli • Brussels Sprouts • Buckwheat • Cabbage • Calendula • Cape Gooseberry • Caraway Seed • Cardoon • Carrot • Cauliflower • Celeriac • Celery • Chamomile • Cherry • Chervil • Chestnut, Sweet • Chickpea (Garbanzo Bean) • Chickweed • Chicory • Chinese Cabbage • Chive • Cilantro • Collard • Coriander Seed • Corn • Corn Salad • Crabapple • Cress • Crosne (Chinese Artichoke) • Cucumber • Currant (Black, Red and White) • Dandelion • Dill • Egg (Chicken) • Eggplant • Elderberry • Endive • Fennel Root, Seed and Leaf • Fig • Flax Seed • French Sorrel • French Tarragon • Garlic Bulb and Scape • Garlic Chives • Geranium Leaf • Goji Berry • Gooseberry • Grape • Greek Oregano • Green Onion (Scallion) • Ground Cherry • Hazelnut • Honey • Horseradish • Kale • Kiwi • Kohlrabi • Lavender • Leek • Lemon (Meyer) • Lemon Balm • Lemon Verbena • Lettuce • Lima Bean • Loganberry • Lovage • Magenta Spreen • Mesclun Mix • Miner's Lettuce • Mint • Mushroom • Mustard Greens and Seed • Nasturtium Seed and Flower • Nectarine • Nettle • Oca (New Zealand Yam) • Onion • Oregano • Oriental Greens • Parcel • Parsley • Parsnip • Pea • Peach • Pear • Pepper • Perpetual Spinach • Plum • Poppy Seed • Potato • Pumpkin • Purslane • Quince • Quinoa • Radicchio • Radish • Raspberry • Rhubarb • Rosehips • Rosemary • Rutabaga • Sage • Salsify • Saskatoon Berry • Sea Kale • Shallot • Silverbeet • Sorrel • Spinach • Sprouted Seeds (Cress, broccoli, mustard, sunflower, bean and pea) • Squash and Blossoms • Strawberry • Strawberry Spinach • Summer Savory • Sunchoke (Jerusalem Artichoke) • Sunflower Seed • Sweet Cicely • Sweet Corn • Sweet Marjoram • Sweet Violet • Swiss Chard • Tayberry • Thyme • Tomatillo • Tomato • Turnip • Wasabi (Japanese Horseradish) • Walnut • Watercress • Winter Savory • Zucchini

HUMAN NUTRITION

"We have a healthcare system that does not care about food, and a food system that does not care about health."

—Wayne Roberts, author of *The No-Nonsense Guide to World Food*

One hundred years ago, our food was grown on small family farms using two strong horses (known as two horsepower). Today one farm machine uses four hundred horsepower, and multitudes of them roll over thousands of acres. Agribusiness aspires to ever-increasing yields and vast profits by taking advantage of cheap fossil fuels. But it is not only quantity and monetary reward that need to be measured.

The human body is both a complex and a miraculous organism, fine-tuned to carry out myriads of specialized functions every moment of its existence. Yet many humans trundle through life taking their body for granted, expecting it to function perfectly, regardless of what they put into it. It takes only a cursory glance to see the consequences for human health of relying on highly processed and adulterated foods grown in depleted soils. Surely, what should be measured are the nutrient levels of the food produced, and what should be taught in schools is basic human nutrition.

"Eater—feeder, consumer, partaker, taster, nibbler, boarder, messer, messmate, breakfaster, luncher, diner, banqueter, feaster, picnicker, diner-out, dainty feeder, connoisseur, gourmet, epicure, trencherman, gourmand, bon viveur, glutton, flesh eater, carnivore, vegetarian, vegan, herbivore."

—*Roget's Thesaurus*

Eating should not be confusing, but after years of conflicting information, changing dietary guidelines and genetic modifications to food, the consumer is no longer sure what is good (or safe) to eat.

Slow Food

In 1986, Carlo Petrini started the Slow Food movement in Rome to safeguard a healthy relationship to food while living in a frenetic, fast-paced world. The focus of Slow Food is on fresh, local, seasonal and sustainable food choices that protect the environment—in a word, *eco-gastronomy*. Since then, the concept of Slow Food has been embraced in more than 150 countries.

The Slow Food movement advocates:

- Slowing down the pace over meals and taking time to savour each morsel.
- Paying attention to food quality.
- Using all our senses—sight, smell, taste, touch and hearing—to practise awareness of the food on our plate.
- Consuming food without guilt.
- Dining with friends and family in a leisurely fashion and spending quality time together while eating.
- Playing music to calm the atmosphere and aid digestion.
- Giving our digestive system a break by eating simple ingredients, and not too many at once.
- Eating smaller portions.
- Keeping the kitchen and dining areas clean and uncluttered.

HEALTHY CHILDREN

Since the 1970s, the number of fast-food restaurants and outlets around the world has more than doubled, with portions increased to supersize. And supersizing is exactly the effect an increased intake of daily calories is having on children, adolescents and adults who regularly eat at these fast-food outlets! Consuming a large percentage of our diet in the form of processed and prepackaged foods puts us at risk of becoming overweight or obese, which is due to the added intake of fats and oils, sugars and salts found in this type of food. The favoured foods of children today are hamburgers, french fries, candy, hot dogs, pizza and pop. Deep-fried foods are loaded with fat and empty calories, and an average can of pop contains 10 teaspoons (50 mL) of sugar.

Cutting calories has been shown to lower weight in the short term, but usually results in binge-eating and gaining back the lost pounds. Diets that are high in protein, low in carbohydrates and low in calories are not safe for developing children and teens. Like adults, they would gain control of their weight more successfully by switching from eating empty calories to embracing a healthier diet based on fruits, vegetables, grains and legumes.

Getting Kids to Eat Good Food

Many children, mostly those between the ages of three and five, experience food aversions, and many parents face a battle of wills around the dinner table as they worry about feeding their children nutritious food. Children eat best in an emotionally positive atmosphere, and nagging and trying to manipulate them into eating does not qualify as one!

Lead by Example

Parents acting as role models can shape their children's preference for foods. Simply feeding your children the same healthy foods you are eating will expose them to a wide variety of tastes and textures. By savouring fruits and vegetables yourself, you will help develop healthy eating patterns in your children. When you eat well, your children learn to eat well, too. When wholesome foods are readily available, it

Nurture your little ones with a healthy diet based on fruits, vegetables, grains and legumes.

encourages most children to choose a well-balanced diet over time. For extra support, get your picky child to eat with kids who are "good eaters" and who enjoy foods your child commonly refuses.

Grow Some Food

Imagine your children's excitement after planting a seed, nurturing it, watching it grow and then harvesting the results. Growing their own food is a great way to support children's acceptance of fruits and vegetables. Gardening also increases children's ability to identify fruits and vegetables, and their knowledge of what's available locally through each season of the year. Most importantly, when you grow your own food, you are empowering your children to do the same throughout their lives.

Choose from a Rainbow of Vegetables

Red: Radishes, sweet peppers and onions
Yellow/orange: Squash, carrots and yams
Purple: Radicchio, eggplant and beets

Green: Kale, spinach and broccoli
Brown: Turnips, parsnips, potatoes and sunchokes

Make Food Fun!

Introduce your kids to the sights and sounds of the local farmers' market, asking them to choose some fruits and vegetables to take home in their basket. How can they resist those ruby-red tomatoes or that chartreuse 'Romanesco' broccoli? When you get home, they can turn colourful carrots into star shapes and broccoli into trees, making eating them even more fun! Pick something from your day's adventure to try growing in your own backyard—your children will learn to love this vegetable for life.

Teach Kids about Cooking

Let your children give you a hand in the kitchen. Children who play a role in preparing fruits and vegetables develop an interest in food, and are excited to eat what they have prepared. For the very best experience, start the lesson by picking the food from the garden.

Children are often more willing to eat vegetables that they've helped harvest.

Teach Kids about Nutrition

Encourage children to learn the value of good nutrition and to understand how important food is for normal growth and development, good health and fitness. Help them make friends with their food, keeping it simple and healthful and part of your family's daily rhythm.

Tips for Happy Eaters

- Serve snacks and meals every three hours.
- Plan a routine to serve meals at the same time every day.
- Limit snack foods before mealtimes.
- Stock the house with healthful options. Keeping unhealthy snacks out of the home is an easy way to eliminate conflicts over food.
- Introduce new tastes gradually. Children may need to see food 20 times before they accept it. Don't give up after only a few attempts!
- If your children will only eat one healthy food, indulge them. They usually move on to something else after a while.
- Try to offer at least one food you know your children like at every meal.
- If children are tired, upset or overexcited, it may not be a good time for them to eat.
- Do not use dessert as a reward for eating the rest of the meal. If a child picks at the meal and will only eat dessert, try to make sure the dessert is a fruit dish rather than a sugary cake or ice cream.
- Accept that sometimes children are hungry and eat a lot. Sometimes they do not want as much food.
- Serve small amounts on small plates and offer more if your children finish their meal.
- Do not pressure a toddler to finish food or drink.
- Teach your children to grow their own food, and help them learn the value of knowing where their food comes from. A simple container or windowsill garden will do the trick if you don't have a yard to work with. Or consider seeking out a patch in your local community garden for a delightful family adventure.

- Include "snackscaping" in your garden plan: peas, strawberries and blueberries are big favourites with most children.
- Daily exercise is also key to a healthy appetite— and in addition to a visit to the park or a bike ride, gardening is a wonderful way to be active and outside.

Q Many families with working parents rely on prepared and processed snacks that have a big appeal to children. Is there an easy alternative to these high-calorie "foods" that are often full of unhealthy fats?

A Here are some great suggestions for convenient snack-food alternatives that you can feel good about giving to your child:
- Applesauce (page 243)
- Chopped Vegetable Sticks
- Flavoured Popcorn (page 19)
- Fresh Fruit
- Fresh Fruit Popsicles (page 183)
- Fruit Compotes (page 76)
- Fruit Leather (page 27)
- Granola (see following recipe)
- Hard-Boiled Eggs
- Homemade Cupcakes (page 177)
- Homemade Soups (see index)
- Hummus (pages 147 and 149)
- Tabouleh (page 159)
- Wraps (pages 126 and 167)
- Yogourt (page 93)

Jeanie's Honey Granola

It only takes 10 minutes to make 10 cups of this nourishing granola.

½ cup (125 mL) raw hazelnuts, chopped

½ cup (125 mL) unsalted raw cashews

½ cup (125 mL) unsalted raw sunflower seeds

½ cup (125 mL) unsalted raw pumpkin seeds

6 cups (1.4 L) rolled oats, large flaked or quick cooking

1 cup (250 mL) wheat germ

½ cup (125 mL) unsweetened coconut (optional)

½ cup (125 mL) flax seeds (optional)

1 tsp (5 mL) cinnamon powder

½ cup (125 mL) vegetable oil

½ cup (125 mL) liquid honey

1 cup (250 mL) of dried fruit—raisins, currants, blueberries, strawberries, cherries

Preheat the oven to 325F (160C).

Stir all the dry ingredients together.

Mix the honey and the oil. Add to the dry mixture and combine well. Spread into two 9 × 13-inch (23 × 33-cm) baking pans.

Place on the middle shelf of the preheated oven and bake for 15 minutes. Turn the granola in the baking pan. Turn the oven down to 225F (105C) and bake for another 20 minutes, until the granola is golden brown.

Remove from the oven and mix in the dried fruit. Allow to cool before storing in an airtight gallon glass jar.

Makes 10 cups (2.5 L)

Popcorn VG* GF

Well, who knew? Organic popcorn is the perfect snack food, being 100 percent unprocessed whole grain. Popcorn contains high levels of polyphenol antioxidants, known to lower cholesterol and fight cancer.

Although popcorn at theatres is smothered in butter and salt, making it high calorie and high fat, popcorn at home presents a new world of possibilities, particularly if you grow the popping corn in your own garden.

¼ cup (60 mL) extra virgin olive or grapeseed oil
1 cup (250 mL) popcorn kernels

Choose a heavy saucepan. Pour in the oil so that it covers the bottom by ¼ inch (5 mm). Heat the oil. Add the popcorn kernels and place the lid on the saucepan. Shake the saucepan to cover the kernels in oil. Let it reheat and as soon as the popping starts, resume shaking the saucepan in a forward-and-back motion.

When there's no more popping, it's ready for your choice of topping(s). Pour the flavoured popped corn into a big bowl and tuck in!

Makes 4 servings

*when using vegan topping choices

Healthy Toppings

- Nutritional yeast (see page 46)
- Vegetable salt (see page 66)
- Gomasio (see page 39)
- Fresh dillweed and butter
- Seaweed flakes with fresh-grated unrefined salt

Grow Your Own Popcorn

It's fun to grow your own organic (non-GM) popping corn. It comes in many varieties and colours—from red to white to yellow to blue. Cobs are generally smaller than sweet corn, and they take longer to mature, but the requirements for cultivation are the same. Popcorn has higher starch content than sweet corn, and to pop, the kernel must contain just the right level of moisture. The time of harvesting and subsequent curing is important—before the first hard frost, when the corn kernels are plump and hard, the cobs should be husked and left to cure for four weeks in a cool place. After this time, test for popping. If the kernels do not pop well, dry for one more week and test again, but do not let them dry until shrivelled. Store inside a dark cupboard in glass jars.

SPRING CLEANING FOR YOUR BODY

Eat Plenty of Fresh Fruits and Vegetables

Nothing beats the zero-mile diet when it comes to spring cleaning your body by eating fruits and vegetables. You're bound to feel the difference when eating organically grown food that has been freshly harvested from garden to kitchen. Spring cleaning with pesticide-laden agrifoods has questionable merit, but nutrient-rich food from your garden or local organic farm seems like a much better fit.

Fruits and vegetables are rich in antioxidants that protect cells from free-radical damage, considered to be the main cause of aging. Eating foods high in antioxidants has been shown to reduce the incidence of cancer and heart disease. Vitamins C, E and B-complex, as well as selenium, zinc and beta carotene, are all essential for detoxification— and found in plentiful supply in fresh fruits and vegetables. Aim for six to eight servings a day, and consider getting a high-quality juicer to make meeting your antioxidant needs even easier.

Eat Lots of Berries

Colourful berries contain potent antioxidant flavonoids called anthocyanins, which protect many

A freezer full of frozen berries is perfect for spring cleaning.

body systems and help regenerate the liver. Include handfuls of such zero-mile crops as blueberries, strawberries, raspberries, blackcurrants, tayberries and blackberries in your diet wherever you can. Use them as toppings with granola to start the day, and add them to refreshing fruit smoothies.

Consume Fibre

Eating lots of fruits and vegetables also means you are eating a high-fibre diet, excellent for the speedy and regular elimination of waste and toxins from the body. Fibre plays a vital role in flushing waste out of the digestive system. For extra fibre, try ground flax seeds, hemp hearts and psyllium husks, and grow these foods in the garden:

Quality Sources of Dietary Fibre

- Apples
- Asparagus
- Broccoli and Brussels Sprouts
- Celery
- Corn
- Dried Peas and Beans
- Eggplant
- Leafy Greens of Turnip, Kale, Chard, Mustard and Collards
- Leeks
- Potatoes
- Romaine Lettuce
- Root Vegetables
- Strawberries and Raspberries (edible seeds)

Think Probiotics

Probiotic foods contain living micro-organisms that recolonize the human digestive tract with beneficial bacteria that synthesize vitamins, absorb nutrients and keep pathogens at bay. Excellent sources are yogourt, kombucha, kefir, miso and fermented (live cultured) vegetables. For good health, eat these foods every day. See page 92 for how to make your own fermented foods.

This five-colour chard provides a vibrant splash in the garden as well as on the dinner plate. Easy to grow from a direct sowing in spring or fall, chard will provide bunches of leafy greens all season long, especially when the soil is fertile. It's best grown in part sun to prevent the plants from bolting to seed.

Think Prebiotics

Prebiotics work synergistically with probiotics by promoting the proliferation of beneficial bacteria in the digestive system. A diet rich in prebiotics feeds intestinal flora. Good sources are organic dandelion greens from your own yard or another reliable pesticide-free source, and radicchio, frisée, endive, onions, asparagus, chicory, sunchokes, garlic, wheat and sprouted wheat—all of which you can grow yourself!

Drink Pure Water and Juices

Pure water—naturally contaminant-free or filtered to remove impurities—eliminates toxins from the bloodstream and flushes waste from cells. For a great liver flush, drink one part garden-fresh juiced fruits or berries diluted with three parts pure water.

PLANTS OF VALUE FOR A SPRING CLEAN

Milk Thistle

Milk thistle (*Silybum marianum*) has been used for two thousand years as a remedy for a variety of ailments, particularly liver, kidney and gallbladder problems. Scientific studies suggest that a flavonoid in milk-thistle seeds, silymarin, protects the liver from toxins by helping the liver to grow new cells and repair itself; it also has antioxidant and anti-inflammatory properties. Silymarin prevents damage from drugs like acetaminophen, which can cause liver damage if taken in high doses.

Wheat Grass

If you can get used to the sickly sweet taste of chlorophyll, there are many benefits to be had from drinking wheat grass (or barley) juice. The juice made from wheat grass and barley is 70 percent chlorophyll and rich in vitamins and minerals. It has been shown to lower the presence of heavy metals in children. The juice of wheat grass and barley is a living food rich in enzymes known to inhibit the activation of carcinogens and retard bacterial growth in the body. Buy organic hard wheat berries for sprouting. TIP: Use a hand-crank juicer to juice the chlorophyll-rich leaves without having to worry about power outages!

It's easy to grow trays of wheat grass on a sunny windowsill.

Nettles

Nettles contain vitamins C, B$_2$ and K, beta carotene, calcium, magnesium, iron and silica. Because they are rich in iron and minerals, they help fight anemia, fatigue, exhaustion and other effects of stress. A meal of nettles provides a perfect spring tonic.

Stinging nettles (*Urtica dioica*) are covered with nearly invisible stinging hairs that produce intense pain, followed by skin irritation. They usually appear in disturbed habitats, moist woodlands and thickets, along rivers and creeks and partially shaded trails. That's where you can look for them in early spring. I am fortunate to have a patch of nettles by the creek running through our property. The string trimmer is the nettle gourmet's best friend. Nettles that have been mown down reliably burst with fresh new growth, and it's the tender tips that are the best.

I don a pair of protective gloves, and grab a bucket and scissors to harvest tender tips of nettles as they emerge. After using tongs and rinsing the nettles, I place them in a steam tray above boiling water and leave them for five minutes. The stinging hairs collapse and the sweet tender greens are like spinach. Enjoy them in Camille's Nettle Pesto (see page 138), or use them in place of chard in Fennel, Chard and Goat Cheese Pie (see page 203).

Nettle Soup

This soup, brimming with iron and minerals, provides a perfect pick-me-up boost following the winter blahs.

4 cups (1 L) tender young nettle tips

2 Tbsp (30 mL) butter

1 onion, chopped

2 large garlic cloves, minced

1 large or 2 smaller leeks, white and tender green parts only, thinly sliced and washed

2 celery stalks, finely chopped

4 cups (1 L) Vegetable Stock with Lovage (see page 60)

1 tsp (5 mL) sea salt

1 tsp (5 mL) fresh-ground pepper

Garnish: **Chopped chives, yogourt**

* if using olive oil instead of butter, and soy yogourt

Handling the nettles with tongs, discard any tough stalks and wash the nettle tips in a large basin of cold water.

Melt the butter in a large saucepan. Add the onion and garlic, then stir in the leek and celery. Cover and sweat gently for 10 minutes, stirring regularly.

Add the vegetable stock, stir in the washed nettles and simmer for 10 minutes, until the nettles are wilted.

Season with salt and pepper to taste. Leave to cool.

Purée the soup in a blender until smooth.

Heat up gently and serve topped with yogourt and chives.

Makes 6 servings

I don't recommend growing nettles in the garden, as they can be a real pain! On our property, nettles grow down by the creek, from where I can harvest tender tips twice a year (with a pair of gloves on). Give the nettles a good wash (using tongs) and steam them lightly. The stinging hairs will collapse.

Dandelion

In Europe, dandelion (*Taraxacum officinale*) is respected as a nutritional and medicinal powerhouse. Its greens are added to salads and used like lettuce. The root is highly regarded as a tonic to detoxify the liver and frequently enjoyed as a coffee substitute (see Herbal Espresso, page 214). The flowers are used to make dandelion wine.

In North America, we are only beginning to discover the benefits of dandelion in the diet. Dandelion root promotes digestion, providing an excellent boost for the absorption of nutritional vitamin and mineral supplements. It is also a source of vitamins A, B and C, important for heart health, as well as zinc, iron and potassium, which means it is often used as a treatment for anemia. Potassium is necessary for proper kidney function and can help lower blood pressure.

Cilantro

Many people do not like the taste of cilantro (*Coriandrum sativum*), saying it tastes metallic. That's interesting, because cilantro is a chelating agent that removes heavy metals—such as mercury, aluminum and lead—stored in fat cells in our bodies. I love the taste of this herb cut fresh from the garden. A 10-ft. (3-m) row provides plenty of cut-and-come-again leaves year-round. Cilantro can be added to salsas, salads, curry and pasta dishes, paninis and Mexican cuisine, and it makes wonderful pesto, too.

EQUIPPING THE KITCHEN

It can be daunting setting up your first kitchen, not just because of all you need, but also because of the prohibitive cost. When I first arrived in Canada from London, I came carrying only what I could cram into a suitcase—needless to say, this did not include cookware. In the beginning, "make do" worked fine, which meant scouring yard sales and bargain basements for cutlery and utensils. I enjoyed hunting for affordable ways of equipping my kitchen with recycled cookware.

I found my number-one cutting implement 30 years ago—a wooden-handled, carbon-steel Chinese cleaver lying in the basement of a rental house I was living in. As soon as I started using it, I knew it would become my favourite kitchen knife, and it still is today. I depend on it for chopping, splitting, mincing and slicing, and love it so much that when the handle finally split, I found someone to fashion a new one.

Over the years I have accumulated an admirable collection of kitchen cookware. I have also amassed enough great cookbooks to absorb different ways of combining ingredients and seasoning food. Learning to cook is like acquiring a new language—once you have mastered the ABCs of ingredients and techniques, it's easy to whip up fantastic meals in no time.

When equipping your kitchen, don't forget the old adage that "you get what you pay for." I have decided to stay away from supporting the disposable, throwaway culture and from searching for the cheapest product. I'd rather save my pennies over time for top-quality, long-lasting utensils that, given proper care, will last a lifetime—and in many cases can even be passed to the next generation.

Cutting Boards

Stay away from plastic cutting boards, which can be toxic, dirty and ugly. Instead, a wooden cutting board, which has natural antibacterial properties, is ideal. Now there are also lightweight Epicurean boards, dishwasher-safe despite being made from pressed paper. Best of all is a hardwood cutting block, or alternatively one of many attractive hardwood cutting boards. Don't treat the wood with olive oil, which becomes sticky and rancid. Rubbing on mineral oil mixed with beeswax regularly is the correct way to keep wood conditioned.

Food Storage Containers

If you use plastic storage containers, ensure they are BPA-free. Bisphenol A (BPA) is an industrial chemical sometimes used to make polycarbonate plastics and epoxy resins since the 1960s. Polycarbonate plastics are often used in food-storage containers, water bottles, baby bottles and cups. Epoxy resins are used to coat the inside of metal products such as food cans and bottle tops.

Research has proven that BPA from containers can seep into food and beverages, and—because it is structurally similar to the hormone estrogen—has been shown to interfere with reproductive development in animals, in addition to being linked to cardiovascular disease, diabetes and obesity in humans. BPA remains controversial and studies are continuing, but food and drug administrations

Choose quality utensils—they will last a lifetime.

A VISIT TO COOK CULTURE

There's no better place to be on a chilly afternoon than at a local kitchenware store. Owner Jed Grieve kindly invited me to drop by his sparkling Victoria shop, Cook Culture, to check out the latest and greatest in cookware—a delightful prospect for this kitchen-gadget geek. Eventually I had to pull away, because in addition to there being so much to learn, there were too many tempting things to buy. Jed reinforced what I already believe: when outfitting a kitchen we should discern what we truly need and buy quality that will last a lifetime—whether purchasing from a kitchenware shop like Cook Culture, or a thrift store or a garage sale.

Jed's good advice about pots and pans? Try to not be tempted to load up on a 10-piece (or more) set, with cookware you will probably never use. Instead, buy 5 top-quality basics—a frying pan, stockpot, large saucepan with inserted steamer basket, small saucepan and Dutch oven. Then collect additional pieces over the years as you find you need them.

Ninety-five percent of all cookware is aluminum-based stainless steel. Clad cookware—aluminum encased by layers of stainless steel—begins with three-ply as the basic quality, and goes up to heavy-duty seven-ply pots that last as long as cast iron. We talked about cast iron versus stainless steel. Although stainless steel is lighter to lift, for some foods cast iron has superior cooking action—for getting the sweetness out of caramelized onions, for example, and for simmering sauces and glazes. A stainless-steel replica, or any other material including ceramic, cannot match a cast-iron Dutch oven.

An enamelled cast-iron Dutch oven has high esthetic value and is easier to clean because it is less porous than plain cast iron—and it will last a lifetime. Good-quality cookware should withstand generations of use. The main reason people buy new cookware, says Jed, is because the esthetic value declines, but as long as overheating has not ruined the pan, a good scrub with an appropriate cleaner should renew lost glamour. He does not advocate non-stick pots and pans, even PTFE-free, noting that when we use quality cookware effectively, there is no sticking.

....

now share this concern and steps have been taken to remove it and reduce human exposure to BPA in the food supply. Tetra Paks and glass containers are free of BPA, so I have replaced all my plastic food-storage containers with glass jars.

Food Processors and Blenders

Electric food processors and blenders take the brunt out of repetitive food-preparation tasks.

Food processors use blades and interchangeable disks in wider bowls that are appropriate for solid or semi-solid foods. A safety device prevents the motor from operating if the bowl or lid isn't properly attached. A tool is provided to push chunks of food through a tube and into the bowl, protecting fingers from the blades. Use a food processor for slicing or chopping vegetables; grinding nuts, seeds and fruit; shredding or grating cheese or vegetables; puréeing; and mixing and kneading dough.

When it comes to food processors, it is all about the motor. It's worth investing $300 to $400 to get a machine that will last a lifetime, particularly as the bowls are replaceable on quality brands. You can scout for recycled machines in thrift shops and garage sales. A friend recently found a food processor with a cracked bowl for five dollars, then simply ordered a new bowl from her local kitchenware store.

The main purpose of a food blender is to purée or liquefy. The addition of liquid is usually required for a blender to be effective. It's perfect for making drinks such as fruit smoothies or (my favourite) raspberry margaritas! A blender also makes wonderful homemade dressings, dips, mayonnaise and soups—and I can't imagine life in the kitchen without one.

A handy little multi-purpose immersion blender is perfect for whipping egg whites or cream, crushing ice, whizzing salsas or bread crumbs, puréeing hot soups right in the pot, or chopping small quantities of nuts or herbs inside the bowl that comes with it.

Juicer

There are two kinds of juicing machines available for home use. Centrifugal juicers finely shred fruits and vegetable and then spin the pulp at high speed to separate the liquid. Masticating juicers, such as my Champion juicer, work at a lower speed to grind fruits and vegetables and use pressure to extract the juice. While often more expensive, masticating machines are more efficient and create a flavourful juice that is higher in fibre, enzymes and vitamins.

You can juice cucumbers, leafy greens, beets, carrots, celery, tomatoes, wheat grass, apples, pears, berries and kiwis from your own garden. Or whip up purées that are perfect for babies. Making nut butter is another possibility, and even if things get sticky, I think it's great to have a champion in the kitchen!

Goldie's Green Goddess Juice VG GF

This vita-mineral boost will perk you up at any time of the day.

1 bunch greens—kale, spinach or chard

3 large carrots, chopped into chunks

5 medium apples, cored and chopped

2–3 Tbsp (30–45 mL) fresh ginger root, to taste

Juice of ½ lemon

Juice together in the given order.

Makes 4 cups (1 L)

Canner

Using a boiling-water canner is a simple way to process a multitude of foods, such as applesauce, tomato sauce, salsa, fruits, berries, chutneys, relishes and pickles. Canning increases the storage life of food for up to a year—until the next harvest! For $30 you can purchase a new boiling-water canner, and because they last forever, you can probably buy a used one for less.

The canner comes with a metal insert tray, which fits up to 7 to 9 quart (1-L) Mason jars, depending on the size of the canner. The tray has handles, which makes lifting jars easy, but you still need oven gloves for the removal stage. Processing a pint (475-mL) jar requires about 15 minutes at a rolling boil, and processing a quart (1-L) jar, about 25 minutes.

Wide-Mouth Funnel

An inexpensive stainless-steel funnel deserves special mention because it enables you to transfer food without spillage. It fits snugly into glass Mason jars, which means you can pour syrups, juices, sauces, chutneys, jam and jellies into them without making a sticky mess—I just love it!

Dehydrator

My thousand-watt dehydrator is my best friend during harvest season. It works overtime as I keep eight stacking trays filled with sliced fruits and vegetables from the garden. I dry wild mushrooms such as chanterelles, as well as apples, pears, plums, figs, grapes, strawberries, currants, tomatoes, peppers and rosehips.

All winter we enjoy fruit compotes and rehydrated vegetables, which also give a vitamin boost to recipes. We add raisins and currants to granola and morning oatmeal. Delicious roll-up fruit leathers can be dried when making jam by simply pouring some of the jam over a special dehydrator tray.

Fresh herbs dry fast, and nothing beats the aroma of flash-dried dill or oregano. For a yield of 1 oz (28 gr) of dried leaves, dehydrate 8 oz (225 gr) of fresh herbs.

Red currants ready for dehydrating or juicing.

Steamer

The stovetop steamer is fast and efficient at extracting juice from soft, garden-fresh fruits such as grapes, currants and berries (i.e. blackcurrants, redcurrants, raspberries, blackberries, blueberries). Because the juice is only heated, not boiled, this simple steaming method preserves much of the vitamin content.

A large stainless-steel juicer costs around $500 new, but I bought a used one from a friend for $100. (This is the kind of utensil that travels well between friends, family and neighbours.)

I have juiced fruits using a steamer insert (with a catchment tray underneath) that came with my cookware.

Grapes being steamed to make juice.

Slow Cooker

A slow cooker or crockpot is a countertop appliance that maintains a low temperature for hours, allowing unattended cooking of casseroles, soups, stews and bean dishes. Slow cookers are making a comeback, and it's no wonder when you consider that dinner can be set to cook before you leave for work so that it is ready upon your return.

Cooking the whole meal in a single pot reduces washing up, and glazed stoneware makes cleaning easy. Food stays warm after the slow cooker is switched off, which means food can be taken to potlucks in slow cookers without reheating. To me all these things make slow cookers wonderful, but the best part is, unlike pressure cookers, they present no danger of sudden explosion!

A basic slow cooker consists of a stoneware insert surrounded by metal housing, which contains an electric heating element. The glass lid sits in a groove in the insert's edge, where condensed vapour collects to provide a seal. A typical slow cooker heats food to 170F (77C) on low, to 200F (93C) on high. The low temperature of slow cooking makes it impossible to burn food even if it is cooked too long.

This spiral slicer turns zucchini into ribbon or spaghettini pasta.

Pasta Machine

I've always had great admiration for cooks who make their own pasta, judging it to be rather a lot of effort. In reality, all you need are flour, eggs and a pasta machine to roll out the dough. The resulting experience of eating fresh homemade pasta is well worth the effort, and won't your dinner guests be impressed? (See Ravioli with Garden Tomato Sauce on page 205.)

Mandoline Slicer

Until I spent $10 on one of these, I had no idea how much fun I was missing! When it comes to vegetables, using a mandoline slicer is the easiest way to get thin, even slices of anise, fennel, carrots, squash, mushrooms, onions or celeriac. This is the tool for delicate layers of delicious flavour inside egg frittatas. Just be sure to look out for the tips of your fingers as you glide ingredients across the razor-sharp blade.

Spiral Slicer (Spiralizer)

You are going to love giving this gadget a whirl, and so will the kids! With it you can change the taste and texture of raw, firm vegetables—such as carrots, celery, cucumber, potatoes, radish, turnip, sunchoke and zucchini—into something new. Make onion rings with no more crying, pommes frites (skinny french fries) by turning potato slices into strips, and pasta dishes and pizza toppings with a zing! When kids make their own novel vegetable shapes, they suddenly enjoy eating veggies in a new "really fun" way.

Zucchini Ribbon "Pasta"

Use a spiral slicer to turn your garden zucchini into ribbons. It's a low-calorie alternative to pasta.

- **2 cups (475 mL) zucchini ribbons or spaghettini**
- **3 Tbsp (45 mL) Bragg Liquid Aminos or tamari soy sauce**
- **2 Tbsp (30 mL) extra virgin olive oil**

Toss the zucchini ribbons with the seasoning and leave to marinate for a few hours. Heat the oil in a wok or frying pan and sauté the zucchini for 5 minutes. Use ribbons in place of pasta, topped with your favourite sauce or pesto.

Makes 2 to 3 servings

* with gluten-free soy sauce or Bragg Liquid Aminos

Garlic Roaster

This terra-cotta baking dish is perfect for roasting garlic, as well as potatoes, yams, quince and sunchokes. A drizzle of olive oil and a sprig of rosemary or thyme are all you need. In less than 30 minutes, you'll have sweet roasted garlic cloves to add to pasta, pizza, soups and sauces, or just to squeeze onto a warm baguette and enjoy.

Roasted Garlic

Roasting garlic reduces its pungency and brings out sweetness. Squeeze the garlic purée out of each clove and spread it onto warm rustic bread. It's delicious at any time of year.

6 large garlic bulbs, tops sliced off to reveal the tips of the cloves

¼ cup (60 mL) extra virgin olive oil

1 tsp (5 mL) sea salt

Sprig of fresh rosemary or thyme

Preheat oven to 400F (205C).

Place the garlic in a terra-cotta garlic roaster (see above) or baking pan. Drizzle with olive oil. Sprinkle the salt over the bulbs and add a sprig of thyme or rosemary.

Bake in the oven for 25 to 30 minutes until the cloves have softened.

Makes 6 servings

Apple and potato peeler.

Apple Peeler

A clever little gadget called an apple peeler makes it a snap to peel, core and slice by simply turning a handle. The ability to do all this work with one action saves considerable time in the preparation of apple pies, applesauce, baked apples and dried apples. You also have the added option of leaving the peel on the apples. Plus an apple peeler can peel and slice potatoes for scalloped or sautéed dishes!

Food Mill

It took me years to finally acquire a quality stainless-steel food mill, but now that I'm able to strain out the seeds that used to get stuck in my teeth, I enjoy raspberry and blackberry jam much more. It's a gadget that comes in handy for a range of purposes, such as removing seeds from puréed rosehips, skins from cooked tomatoes and peels from apples. It's especially good for making vegetable and fruit purées that are perfect for babies or elderly people with eating difficulties.

Top Tips for Greater Energy Efficiency in the Kitchen

- Stock less food in the fridge and the freezer so that you can turn down the temperature setting.
- Don't leave refrigerator and oven doors open to lose heat. Keep them closed as much as possible.
- Whenever possible, use small appliances—such as a toaster oven or countertop convection oven—instead of the stove oven.
- Defrost food in the fridge or at room temperature (never in the microwave or under running water).
- Use pots and pans with tight-fitting lids.
- Use pots and pans the same size as the burner.
- Recycle old appliances and replace those you depend on with new energy-efficient ones.
- Buy high-quality cookware that will last a lifetime. Cast-iron cookware can be passed down through generations, and it doesn't need to be expensive. You can find good cast-iron frying pans, griddles, pots and Dutch ovens dirt cheap at thrift stores.
- Use a large bowl or basin to save water when you wash dishes. Don't pour water down the drain if you can use it for watering plants or for other cleaning chores.
- Use a large bowl or basin to wash fruits and vegetables so that you do not have to leave the tap running.
- Avoid excessive food wastage by cooking only what you need if it isn't good as a leftover. And if you have leftovers, be thankful that you won't have to cook the next day when leftovers often taste even better!

THE SHOPPING LIST

Stocking the Kitchen

Mindful eating and consuming—referred to as eco-gastronomy by the Slow Food movement—can change the world. When we aspire to rightful living, we need to be aware of food miles for the food we are not able to grow ourselves and whether or not the food is "fair trade" for the producer. And when we aspire to healthful eating, we can begin by stocking the kitchen with the best choices possible. Perhaps it's time to put your kitchen on a diet, and to get rid of ingredients that are questionable in terms of being wholesome, nutritious and unadulterated?

"Don't eat anything your grandmother wouldn't recognize as food."

—Michael Pollan

Put Your Kitchen on a Diet

- Get rid of the deep fryer!
- Avoid factory-farmed meat high in saturated fat that raises LDL (bad) cholesterol.
- Cut out processed carbohydrates such as white bread and white flour products. Instead choose whole grains and fewer products made from refined flour.
- Eliminate foods high in sodium, fat or sugar.
- Keep canned foods out of the cupboard (especially cans with BPA lining).
- Avoid hydrogenated oils and trans fats, and vegetable oils such as safflower, corn, sunflower, cottonseed and canola. Use cold-pressed, extra virgin olive oil and virgin coconut oil as much as possible.
- Avoid processed and refined foods with artificial colours and preservatives, MSG and additives in general. Avoid junk foods, frozen foods, fried foods and candy bars.
- Avoid all artificial sweeteners.
- Plan to drink filtered water, fresh-squeezed juices and black or green teas throughout the day, and avoid purchasing sugary drinks such as soda pops, colas, powder and power drinks.
- Eat regular servings of fresh fruits and vegetables every day. I believe there's nothing better for you than the fruits and vegetables you grow for yourself, because only then can you be fully assured that this food has been grown nutritiously in organic soil, free from chemical fertilizers, herbicides, pesticides and fungicides. Plus, all the tender, loving care you poured into your garden comes back to feed you in so many other ways. The next-best fruits and vegetables for you are those from a local certified organic farmer or a farmer in transition to organic, because you can trust that this food will also nourish you, and at the same time that it will nourish the local economy and the next generation of farmers who will feed us in the future.
- Keep lots of washed veggies and greens handy in the refrigerator so you eat more high-fibre foods.
- Place a fruit basket on the table and keep it filled with what's in season.
- Stock the pantry with whole grains, dried beans, nuts and seeds.
- Renew your culinary herbs and spices once a year, preferably from your own garden whenever possible.
- Stock the best-quality, cold-pressed, unfiltered oils for flavouring instead of salt.
- Buy quality sea salt for when you do need it, and experiment with artisan salts.
- Put glass jars of healthy ingredients—such as quinoa, brown rice and dried fruit—where they are convenient to access.
- Keep your blender handy to make fruit shakes and green smoothies.
- Go crazy for leftovers—soups, casseroles, beans, grains and sprouts are perfect for a healthy snack or meal anytime.
- Supplement your diet with such superfoods as quinoa, seaweed, hemp seeds, goji berries, broccoli sprouts, fermented foods and wild mushrooms.

Buying in Bulk

In the 1970s, I worked as a coordinator of a member-owned storefront food co-operative in Vancouver called Marginal Market. Six hundred households owned the store, where members decided what foods would be stocked, and each member volunteered to work in the store two hours a month. My job was to order the food and direct the "workers" on their shifts. Keeping overhead costs to a minimum allowed all of us to eat healthy organic food at just above wholesale cost. That's when I learned the value of buying food in bulk, and since then I have never let recycled storage jars pass me by! Buying clubs are making a comeback, and perhaps storefront co-ops will, too.

Using recycled glass jars is a great way to store bulk dried beans and pulses.

CERTIFIED ORGANIC FOOD

Standards vary by country, but in general, food labelled as organic must follow these principles:

- Crops grown without synthetic pesticides, herbicides, fumigants, chemical fertilizers or sewer sludge
- Livestock raised without synthetic hormones and with minimal antibiotic use, incorporating animal husbandry practices that support the health and behavioural needs of livestock
- No genetically modified ingredients or cloned animals
- Use sustainable farming practices to promote long-term soil fertility and biological diversity; recycle and reuse resources
- Process without ionizing radiation, artificial preservatives, trans fats, artificial colours, synthetic flavours or artificial sweeteners
- Organic certification requires that farmers develop and follow detailed farm plans, and be inspected regularly to ensure they follow the requirements set forth. Those that do not, cannot display the organic logo.

Healthy Grains

- Amaranth
- Barley
- Buckwheat
- Cornmeal
- Kamut
- Millet
- Oats
- Quinoa
- Rice
- Rye
- Spelt
- Triticale Wheat

Grains are an excellent source of dietary fibre, such minerals as calcium, iron, magnesium and zinc, and vitamins E and B-complex.

Whole grains cannot be eaten directly from the field; they have to be milled, ground, cracked and/or rolled. As the majority of a grain's nutrients are found in the germ and bran, processed grain does not deliver the same balance of nutrients found in the original plant.

Over the years, I have experimented with growing various grains at The Garden Path, and have been delighted to discover that I can produce small quantities for a zero-mile diet. Amaranth, quinoa, wheats, millet, oats, rye, barley and buckwheat all grow well from a scattering of seed over fertile soil in late spring. The grain plants are very ornamental and easy to grow, but of course we would need farmers' fields full of grains to meet our year-round needs. Still, it's empowering to grow what we can!

How to Cook Grains

Add two to three times as much water or vegetable stock to the grain and bring to the boil. Reduce the heat, cover and simmer until the water has been absorbed and the grains are tender for eating. Optional: Add seasonings such as Bragg Liquid Aminos or tamari soy sauce, chopped herbs, spices or dried vegetable flakes to the water before cooking. TIP: To enhance the flavour of whole grains, sauté them first in a little oil for a few minutes until coated. Then add the liquid and other ingredients.

Perfect Quinoa

²/₃ cup (160 mL) quinoa, well rinsed
1 ¹/₃ cups (315 mL) water

Bring the grains and the water to a boil, turn down the heat to very low and put the lid on the saucepan. Simmer for 15 minutes and then remove from the stovetop. Leave the lid on for another 10 minutes and lift off to fluffy perfection!

Makes 1 cup (250 mL)

Quinoa (Chenopodium quinoa) is an easy-to-grow plant that can be direct-seeded or transplanted into the garden, and is happiest in part sun. Space plants 18 inches (45 cm) apart to allow for fully mature seed heads. Thresh these to release the seeds and spread them out to dry. Before eating, wash seeds thoroughly to remove their bitter, soapy coating. The leaves of young plants also make tasty additions to salads.

How to Store Grains

Grains are negatively affected by heat and moisture, and they can become rancid in storage—so they are best kept in a cool, dark place. Purchase grains from an outlet with a high turnover of stock, and in quantities you will consume within a year.

Why Soak Grains?

The bad news about grains is that they contain phytic acid, an anti-nutrient that interferes with the assimilation of vitamins and minerals. The good news is that soaking or sprouting whole unmilled grains breaks down phytic acid, and also converts starch into simple sugars that the body can digest more easily. Different grains contain varying levels of phytic acid and phytase (an enzyme that neutralizes phytic acid), and the required time for soaking varies. Tiny grains such as amaranth, quinoa and millet, or processed grains like couscous and bulgur wheat, absorb water much faster, so can be soaked or simmered for 15 to 20 minutes to achieve the same effect.

Amaranth Grits

Try this easy simmering recipe for tiny amaranth grains and serve accompanied by Easy Slow Cooker Beans (see page 38) and Krunchy Kale Salad (see page 226) or plain steamed greens. TIP: Amaranth absorbs water better if the salt is left out until after cooking.

2½ cups (600 mL) Vegetable Stock with Lovage (see page 60)

1 cup (250 mL) raw amaranth grain

1 garlic clove, minced

1 medium onion, finely chopped

1 Tbsp (15 mL) sea salt or tamari soy sauce to taste

2 fresh large tomatoes, chopped

Bring the stock, amaranth, garlic and onion to the boil. Reduce heat and simmer covered for about 20 minutes until most of liquid is absorbed. Stir well. The grits should be crunchy but not hard.

Add sea salt or tamari soy sauce to taste and garnish with the fresh chopped tomatoes.

Makes 4 servings

* with gluten-free soy sauce

Amaranth is very ornamental and easy to grow.

Dried Beans, Peas and Pulses

- Black Beans
- Garbanzo Beans (Chickpeas)
- Kidney Beans
- Lentils
- Pinto Beans
- Soup Peas
- Soybeans
- Split Peas

Beans, peas and pulses are an inexpensive way to eat, popular in many cultures throughout the world because they contain essential amino acids that when combined with grains and/or dairy provide complete protein. Extremely low in fat, they are mineral-rich in magnesium, iron, zinc, potassium and molybdenum, and are an important source of B vitamins.

Nothing matches the flavour of homegrown dried legumes, but as they require a lot of space to grow a sufficient quantity, dried legumes are also often purchased prepackaged or from the bulk bin section. Buy from stores with a high turnover to ensure maximum freshness and flavour. You can also find canned beans, peas and pulses (preferably BPA-free and without salt or additives). See Bisphenol A (page 24).

Why You Should Soak Dried Beans, Peas and Pulses

All legumes contain phytates, also known as phytic acid, an anti-nutrient that binds up minerals in the gastrointestinal tract. To improve digestibility (less gas!) of beans and maximize their high nutrient value, they need to be soaked before cooking to remove the phytates with the discarded water. It is not necessary, though, to soak lentils, split peas or dried peas.

How to Cook Beans

Before washing, spread the beans out on a light-coloured surface and remove any small stones or damaged beans. Rinse the beans under cold running water to wash away dust and debris from storage. Place in a saucepan that allows for expansion, cover with cold water and leave to soak overnight or for 8 to 12 hours. Use the soaking liquid to water your houseplants, and start with fresh water for cooking.

Bring the water and beans to the boil and reduce to a simmer, partially covering the pot for the prescribed amount of time. If foam develops, skim it off during simmering. Do not add salt until after the beans have been cooked. Adding it earlier makes the beans tough and increases cooking time. Add salt only during the last half hour of cooking, after the beans are soft.

How to Store Beans

Store dried beans, peas and pulses in airtight containers in a cool, dark place, where they will keep for up to a year. If purchasing at different times, store separately, as stages of dryness vary and affect the cooking time required. Cooked beans, peas and pulses keep fresh in the refrigerator for about three days in a covered container.

Beans – 1 cup dried beans (250 mL), presoaked*	Simmer in Water	Time
Soybeans	4 cups (1 L)	2 hours
Garbanzo Beans	3 cups (700 mL)	1½ hours
Pinto Beans	3 cups (700 mL)	2 hours
Kidney Beans**	3 cups (700 mL)	1½ hours
Black Beans	3 cups (700 mL)	1½ hours

* 1 cup (250 mL) dry beans yields approximately 2½ cups (600 mL) cooked beans.

** must have 15 minutes at a rolling boil

Easy Slow Cooker Beans VG GF

Vegan, gluten-free and low fat, these beans make a savoury side dish and are very handy to have around at mealtime.

3 cups (700 mL) presoaked pinto beans (see How to Cook Beans, page 37)

7 cups (1.65 L) water

1 large onion, diced

2 Tbsp (30 mL) ground cumin

2 tsp (10 mL) chili pepper flakes

2 tsp (10 mL) chili powder

3 large garlic cloves, chopped

1 tsp (5 mL) fresh-ground black pepper

1 whole dried pepper—ancho or jalapeno

Combine the presoaked and rinsed beans and all the other ingredients in a slow cooker.

Cover and cook on medium-high heat for 6 to 8 hours.

Store the beans in their cooking liquid in the refrigerator.

Makes 10 to 12 servings

Pinto beans.

Try growing giant sunflowers and dry the mature heads for seeds (before the birds get them!).

Seeds

- Flax Seeds
- Hemp Seeds
- Pumpkin Seeds
- Sesame Seeds
- Sunflower Seeds

Packed with protein, healthy oil, vitamins and minerals, seeds add a nutty crunch wherever they are used. Flax, hemp and pumpkin seeds are all rich sources of healthy omega-3 fatty acids. Similar to grains and legumes, always purchase seeds from an outlet with a high turnover of stock.

Gomasio (Sesame Salt)

Sesame seeds are tiny white or black seeds that have been used as a source of food and oil around the world for thousands of years. The flavour of sesame seeds is improved by toasting them to give them a distinct nuttiness, which enlivens grain, noodle and vegetable dishes when sprinkled liberally over them. I love the effect gomasio has on a simple bowl of cooked rice.

⅔ cup (160 mL) white sesame seeds
2 Tbsp (30 mL) sea salt

Toast the sesame seeds in a cast-iron skillet at medium-high heat until the seeds start to pop and smell fragrant. Grind the toasted seeds with the salt in a suribachi or pestle and mortar, or ¼ cup (60 mL) at a time in a coffee grinder. Store tightly covered in a cool place.

Makes approximately ½ cup (125 mL)

SPROUTING SEEDS

Sprouted seeds are powerhouses of nutrition that strengthen the immune system by providing the greatest amount of vitamins, minerals, proteins and enzymes of any food per unit of calorie, and in a form that is easy to digest. Best of all, this wonder food is inexpensive to buy and does not require special equipment. Prepackaged blends of seeds are available for less than five dollars. I save extra seeds from the garden for sprouting, because almost any whole natural seed, bean or grain will sprout. My peas, sunflowers, radish, broccoli, mustard and cress seeds all make great-eating sprouts when germinated.

Did You Know?

Research shows that eating 4 oz (112 gr) of mixed broccoli, radish, alfalfa and clover sprouts every day for two weeks protects against cancer. Broccoli sprouts in particular are known to contain high concentrations of a cancer-fighting compound called sulforaphane.

How to Sprout Seeds

Fill a wide-mouth quart glass jar with seed. (Use the chart as a guide to quantity.) For larger amounts, use a gallon glass jar.

Cover seeds with water and soak for a few hours or overnight.

Place a screen of fine mesh (available from any hardware store) over the mouth of the jar, using an elastic band or metal ring. TIP: Make sure the screen is firmly in place so you do not inadvertently wash your seeds down the drain when rinsing!

Drain off the soaking water. TIP: Use it to water your houseplants.

Invert the jar in a bowl or on a rack at a 30-degree angle to allow excess water to run off, and place in bright light (but not direct sunlight).

Continue to rinse the seeds twice a day, keeping them at a 30-degree angle afterward to allow excess water to run off, until the sprouts are ready to eat (as indicated by the chart or your personal preference).

To remove the hulls and any unsprouted seeds, tip the ready sprouts into a large stainless-steel bowl and fill it with cold water. The hulls and seeds that did not germinate will float, and the sprouts will sink. Scoop off the floating stuff—I use a tea strainer. Drain the water and return the rinsed sprouts to their jar (or two, if necessary) and invert once again to drain off excess water. They are now ready to eat.

To store, replace the mesh screen with a metal lid, secure with a metal band and keep in the refrigerator for up to two weeks.

How to Sprout Seeds on Cloth

Now you can purchase mats made from compressed wheat grass or coir (coconut fibre) that work very well for sprouting larger seeds, such as buckwheat, peas, unhulled sunflower, wheat or barley.

Soak buckwheat or sunflower for 12 hours; wheat, peas and barley for 8.

Line the sprouting tray with a soaked cloth, and spread the soaked seeds evenly over it. Put the tray in bright light for 5 to 8 days; on the windowsill works well. Keep the tray moist at all times, checking daily to see if it needs watering or misting.

Young sprouts 4 inches (10 cm) tall are ready for harvesting with scissors.

Sprouting Chart

Soak seeds overnight or as required before sprouting (see table).

Sprouts grow best in even temperature and light. The exception is mung beans, which are grown in complete darkness to prevent bitterness. They should be placed in a drainable tray and will need rinsing twice a day.

Note: Soybeans contain a harmful enzyme and should not be eaten raw. Always steam or sauté before eating.

JAR

	Quantity	Time	Harvest Length
Alfalfa, Broccoli, Radish, Red Clover	2 Tbsp (30 mL)	4–5 days	1½ inch (4 cm)
Garbanzo Beans	1 cup (250 mL)	4 days	½ inch (1 cm)
Lentils, Whole	½ cup (125 mL)	4 days	½ inch (1 cm)
Peas, Whole	½ cup (125 mL)	4–5 days	½ inch (1 cm)

TRAY

Mung Beans	½ cup (125 mL)	3–4 days	3 inches (7.5 cm)
Sunflower (Unhulled)	½ cup (125 mL)	5–8 days	3 inches (7.5 cm)
Wheat Grass	1 cup (250 mL)	5–8 days	2 inches (5 cm)

Nuts

- Almonds
- Brazil Nuts
- Cashews
- Hazelnuts (Filberts)
- Macadamia Nuts
- Peanuts
- Pecans
- Pine Nuts
- Pistachios
- Walnuts

Organically grown nuts are a great source of protein, fat, vitamins, minerals and many other life-enhancing nutrients. They are enjoyed raw or toasted, salted and unsalted, and are useful in desserts and baked goods, as well as many savoury dishes. It's unfortunate that most nuts are imported, but they provide such a valuable contribution to a healthy diet that it's worth making them an exception to the food-miles rule.

In *The Zero-Mile Diet: A Year-Round Guide to Growing Food*, I talk about growing several species of nut trees—hazelnut (*Corylus avellana*), sweet chestnut (*Castanea sativa*) and walnut (*Juglans* spp.). If you have the space, plant a nut tree! Or it may be worth doing some research to find possible sources of locally grown nuts of these same species to save the food miles.

Nut Allergies

Peanuts, walnuts, Brazil nuts, hazelnuts and almonds are known to be common allergens, and can trigger a life-threatening reaction called anaphylaxis. Sufferers must take every precaution to avoid eating any trace of nuts.

Roasting Nuts

Roasted nuts are more difficult to digest than soaked nuts, and roasting may destroy nutrient content and digestive enzymes. However, roasting adds crispness and flavour to bland nuts, particularly hazelnuts and peanuts, which makes a big difference to recipes they are used in. The easiest way to roast nuts is in a preheated oven at 375F (190C) for 5 to 15 minutes, turning halfway through. You can also dry-toast nuts in a preheated cast-iron skillet for 2 to 4 minutes, stirring until the nuts have browned slightly.

Why You Should Soak Nuts

Nuts contain the anti-nutrient phytic acid, which should be removed by soaking in order to get the most benefit from the bounty of nutrients nuts offer.

For people who experience problems digesting nuts (and even for folks who don't), soaking shelled raw nuts deals effectively with the enzyme inhibitors and makes them more easily digested. Raw, soaked nuts are the best for health, and as with introducing any new food, it's best to increase consumption in small increments, thus preventing a strain on the digestive system.

Soak nuts anywhere from the minimum time of 20 minutes to overnight in the refrigerator. If you keep nuts soaking in the refrigerator, change the water every 2 days so they don't spoil. Soaking nuts in plastic is not recommended, as plastic can leach into the water and food. Choose glass containers with airtight lids.

Make Your Own Nut Butters

Beware of shop-bought nut butters that may contain hydrogenated oil and sugar. You can easily make your own by placing ½ cup (125 mL) of shelled nuts in a food processor and blending them until they are finely and evenly ground. Then pour 2 Tbsp (30 mL) vegetable oil into the processor and continue to blend to a coarse or smooth paste. Store nut butter in an airtight jar in the refrigerator.

How to Store Nuts

With the exception of peanuts, nuts are the large seeds of mature trees, with hard shells and energy stored as fat, which makes them high in calories and best eaten in moderation. This high fat content also makes nuts susceptible to going rancid, so buy them in smaller quantities for quick consumption. The shelf life of nuts can be extended by storing them in the refrigerator in airtight containers. Shelled nuts will store for up to four months; unshelled, for up to eight. You can also keep them in the freezer for up to two years.

Baked Oatmeal with Nuts and Fruit

Topped with a little extra maple syrup and berries, either fresh or from the freezer, this reminds me of French toast—perfect for serving a brunch crowd. Soaking the grains and nuts makes this an even more nutritious way to start the day. Oats are a good source of B vitamins, including folate, and are rich in minerals, including phosphorus, magnesium, manganese, iron and zinc.

1 lb (454 gr) steel cut oats

1 cup (250 mL) hazelnuts

2 Tbsp (30 mL) plain yogourt

1 tsp (5 mL) sea salt

6 eggs

2 cups (475 mL) milk

¼ cup (60 mL) maple syrup

½–1 cup (125–250 mL) dried fruit such as raisins, cherries or currants

1 Tbsp (15 mL) cinnamon powder

½ tsp (2.5 mL) grated nutmeg

¼ cup (60 mL) grapeseed oil

Pour the oats and the nuts into a large mixing bowl, and add enough water to completely submerge. Add the salt and yogourt and stir to blend. Allow to soak, covered, overnight in a warm place. (On top of the woodstove as it is dying out is perfect!)

The next morning, preheat the oven to 350F (175C). Oil a 9 × 13-inch (23 × 33-cm) baking pan.

In a colander, drain oats and nuts to remove extra liquid. Place them back into the mixing bowl.

Beat the eggs, milk and maple syrup together.

Pour over the soaked oats and nuts, stirring well. Gently fold the dried fruit, spices and oil into the mixture. Pour into the greased baking pan, smoothing with a spatula.

Bake for 45 minutes until the oatmeal is golden brown on top and a toothpick inserted in the centre comes out clean. If it needs longer to set, turn off the oven, leave the door slightly ajar, and leave the pan in the oven for another 30 minutes. Allow to cool for 10 minutes before serving.

Makes 8 servings

* Oats are gluten-free but are sometimes exposed to gluten during processing. If concerned, check the label to make sure they are certified gluten-free.

HEALTHY OILS AND FATS

Oils and fats come from a variety of sources: cereals such as corn; fruits such as olives; nuts such as walnuts, peanuts, almonds and hazelnuts; and seeds such as flax, hemp, safflower, sunflower, sesame and rapeseed (canola). They are extracted by pressing (crushing) or by heat extraction. The highest-quality oils, called extra virgin, are obtained from the first cold pressing, with particles lightly filtered, and contain no chemical additives. You pay more for the best-quality oils, but it's worth it in terms of flavour and nutritional benefit.

For Cooking

- Butter
- Coconut Oil
- Grapeseed Oil
- Olive Oil
- Palm Oil

For Salads and Raw Use

- Extra Virgin Olive Oil
- Flax Oil
- Grapeseed Oil
- Sesame Oil
- Unrefined Oils such as Hemp, Walnut or Almond

Oils to Avoid

- All hydrogenated and partially hydrogenated (trans fat) oils
- Refined oils that have been heat processed and are also high in omega-6 fatty acids, such as soy, corn, safflower, sunflower and canola (rapeseed)

JUST REMEMBER THIS

- Bad fats (saturated and trans fats) increase bad cholesterol.

- Good fats (monounsaturated and polyunsaturated) reduce bad cholesterol.

- A good balance of essential omega-3 and omega-6 fatty acids in the diet is essential for growth and maintenance of cell membranes as well as physical and emotional well-being. Omega-3 fatty acids generally reduce inflammation, whereas omega-6 fatty acids tend to promote inflammation.

How to Store Oils

The best way to safeguard the nutritive value of oil is to keep it cool until opening, 39F (4C) to 72F (22C), in a dark cupboard. Once opened, oils are best stored in the refrigerator if not consumed within 60 days. The shelf life for refined oils is 14 to 20 months; for unrefined oils, 10 to 14 months. You can test for rancidity by nose.

Vinegar

For the best results in flavour, use only high-quality vinegars. Vinegar is used as a preservative in pickles and condiments, and is a key ingredient in marinades and dressings. See Herbal Vinegars (page 67).

Wine Vinegar

Slow-fermentation processes that avoid heat make the smoothest-flavoured wine vinegar. The quality of the vinegar depends on the standard of the wine it is made from.

Balsamic Vinegar

Balsamic vinegar adds a complex, tangy flavour to everything it touches. It's great in barbecue marinades, as well as tossed with a drizzle of olive oil over kale greens.

Malt Vinegar

Malt vinegar is made from beer and has a harsh, mouth-puckering flavour that makes it unsuitable for salad dressings but great on french fries!

Rice Vinegar

Rice vinegar is generally a clear brown colour, but it can also be red, white or black. Japanese rice vinegar is sweet and often used to flavour rice in sushi. It also is added to many other dishes. Chinese rice vinegar is usually sharper in taste.

Cider Vinegar

Apple cider vinegar is stronger in flavour than wine vinegar and pale brown with a slightly fruity flavour. It has a shelf life of five years and can be stored at room temperature. Apple cider vinegar is a natural detoxifying product that prohibits the growth of bacteria, yeast and fungi within the intestinal tract. It also purifies the blood and revitalizes the immune system. It has gained in notoriety and is now the base for many diets and detoxification plans.

Raspberry Vinegar

What a difference a few raspberries make to white wine vinegar—and what a difference raspberry vinegar makes to salad dressings and sauces!

½ cup (125 mL) raspberries
2 cups (475 mL) white wine vinegar

Lightly crush raspberries and mix with white wine vinegar. Leave to steep 2 to 3 weeks. Strain and bottle. Keep in a cool, dark cupboard.

Makes 2 cups (475 mL)

SEASONINGS

Soy Sauce

Soy sauce is made by combining crushed soybeans with wheat, salt and water, and adding a yeast-based culture called koji. This mixture is left to naturally ferment for between six months and three years. It's best to purchase soy sauce that has been naturally brewed, because otherwise it may have been prepared with chemicals to speed up the fermentation process, and also may contain other additives.

There are different types of soy sauce: light and dark, wheat and wheat-free. Darker soy sauce is sweeter with stronger flavour, making it a good choice for marinades, stir-fries and sauces. Light soy sauce tends to be saltier, and is thinner in consistency. Tamari soy sauce is less salty with a more complex flavour. Both soy sauce and tamari contain wheat, but wheat-free versions of tamari are available for gluten-free diets. Shoyu is a modern-day brewed soy sauce with a balanced taste that is sharper than tamari due to stronger alcoholic fermentation.

Salt

We need only a moderate amount of sodium in our diets. It's surprising to discover that three-quarters of the salt we need occurs naturally in the food we consume. Used in small quantities, salt enhances the flavour of food, and I encourage you to experiment with many of the fine rock and sea salts that are now being introduced to supermarket shelves, instead of choosing refined salt with additives.

A high-sodium diet raises the risk of high blood pressure, hypertension and water retention, and results in increased risk for cardiovascular disease and stroke. The average North American consumes 3,400 milligrams salt daily (about 1½ tsp), much more than the recommended 1,500 milligrams (less than ½ tsp) health authorities recommend. People at risk of health problems from salt should make 1,500 milligrams (less than ½ tsp) their upper limit.

WAYS TO REDUCE SALT IN YOUR DIET

· Always taste your food before adding salt.

· Add salt late in the cooking process, to allow food to release flavour during cooking. Grains do not need to be salted if served with a seasoned sauce or a condiment such as Bragg Liquid Aminos or soy sauce.

· Try herbs, lemon juice, garlic and ginger instead of salt. Use spices such as black pepper, cinnamon and turmeric, or add chili peppers or lemon juice to stimulate the palate. TIP: Finish food with a drizzle of artisan oil, such as almond or walnut, instead of salting.

· Skip the added salt by eating less bread and experiment with whole grain dishes instead. Bread (even whole grain) is one of the largest contributors of sodium to our diets because we eat so much of it!

· Read and compare labels, and look for products with less than 300 milligrams of sodium per serving. Some foods high in sodium, such as breakfast cereals, bakery goods and energy drinks, may not taste salty.

· Beware of high sodium in processed seasonings, stocks and sauces. Many forms of sodium are used in food processing— monosodium glutamate (MSG), sodium citrate, sodium bicarbonate and sodium alginate. Choose reduced-sodium versions of traditional condiments or use salted seasonings sparingly. Bragg Organic Sprinkle Seasoning is a 50-year-old salt-free recipe of natural herbs and spices that adds flavour to most recipes.

· Choose fresh meat and vegetables. Processed and cured meats typically have more salt than fresh meats, and canned vegetables have more salt than fresh.

· Check the labels of canned foods. Draining and rinsing canned foods dramatically cuts their sodium level. Compare brands, choosing those with the lowest levels of sodium.

· Choose unsalted nuts or popcorn instead. Know which snack foods are high in sodium and eat them sparingly.

Liquid Aminos

Containing 16 amino acids, Bragg Liquid Aminos is a liquid protein concentrate made from non-GM soybeans and purified water that has not been heated. It provides great taste and nutrition when added to a wide variety of recipes for soups, dressings, spreads, grains and smoothies.

Nutritional Yeast

If you've eliminated meat from your diet, or are a vegan or vegetarian, nutritional yeast fortified with B_{12} is a valuable addition to your diet. Simply sprinkle 1 Tbsp (15 mL) a day onto your food for your daily dose of B_{12}. Nutritional yeast can also be used as a condiment, and its cheese-like flavour makes it a great low-sodium, cholesterol-free, gluten-free, vegan addition to recipes and foods.

A group learns to identify seaweed on French Beach, Vancouver Island.

Sea Vegetables

Around the world, more than 160 species of sea vegetables are consumed in traditional diets, yet in North America we are only beginning to realize their extraordinary nutritional and medicinal benefits. Seaweed is one of the most powerful foods on Earth, containing vitamins and minerals vital to good health, as well as unique compounds that fight disease, boost immunity, cleanse the body of pollution and keep the skin youthful and glowing.

All seaweeds are edible, but there are only 40 species palatable to us. Many seaweeds contain alginic acid, agar and carrageen, which are jelly-like substances used as stabilizers and thickeners in processed foods such as dressings, syrups, ice creams, desserts, pie fillings and soups.

If you are fortunate enough to live by the ocean, you can harvest your own. Seaweeds should only be gathered from beaches away from sources of pollution. The seaweed collector should make every effort to take plants that are already detached, and avoid specimens that have faded, as they are in the process of decaying. If you do not live by the seaside, you can purchase dried seaweed at the supermarket.

As with any new food being introduced to the diet, it is best done in small increments. A great way to begin is to powder raw, untreated, dried seaweed into flakes, and add them to green smoothies, soups, salads, noodle and grain dishes immediately before eating. Uncooked seaweed adds the best benefit, because the active enzymes are preserved. When soaked, dried seaweed reconstitutes to 10 times its size, so you don't need much to begin with.

Seaweeds should only be harvested from beaches away from sources of pollution. The seaweed collector should make every effort to take plants that are already detached, and avoid specimens that have faded, as they are in the process of decaying.

Arame (Brown Seaweed)

Sold in delicate thin strips, arame has a mild sweet flavour, and is a good choice for the beginner. It needs to be soaked before using if added to raw-food dishes, but can be tossed dried into cooked dishes.

Hijiki (Brown Seaweed)

A thicker version of arame, with stronger flavour, hijiki needs to be soaked before using with raw-food dishes. Only a little is needed because it expands considerably once soaked. It requires longer cooking than most sea vegetables.

Kelp (Brown Seaweed)

Kelp grows in sub-tidal waters with thick round bulbs, from which numerous flat rubbery blades are suspended. These blades have a strong, salty sweet flavour. See Miso Seaweed Soup (page 221).

Kombu (Brown Seaweed)

Usually sold dried in strips, kombu has a very strong flavour, and is best added to dishes that are cooked slowly, such as soups and stocks. It is an essential ingredient in the popular Japanese soup stock dashi. TIP: Adding a small strip of kombu to beans while they are cooking makes them more tender and increases their digestibility.

Wakame (Brown Seaweed)

Wakame looks very similar to kelp, but when soaked changes colour to green. Mild in flavour, it has many uses: add to soups and salads, or roast it and crumble flakes into dishes as a seasoning.

Nori (Red Seaweed)

With a delicate texture and mild flavour, nori is sold in packets of thin, black sheets, and is one of the few sea vegetables that do not require soaking. Nori is used in Japanese cuisine wrapped around vinegared rice to make sushi.

Dulse (Red Seaweed)

With chewy-textured flat fronds and a spicy flavour when cooked, dulse needs to be soaked before adding to dishes. It can also be roasted and crumbled as a garnish.

Ulva (Sea Lettuce)

A bright-green seaweed found worldwide in calm waters and tidal pools, sea lettuce can be harvested early to late summer. It has delicate, very thin ruffled fronds that look like frilly lettuce leaves, and a mild pungent flavour.

SWEETENERS

Honey

"When I add a spoon of honey to my tea, I give thanks to a dozen bees for the work of their whole lives. When my finger sweeps the final drop of sweetness from the jar, I know we've enjoyed the nectar from over a million flowers. This is what honey is—the souls of flowers, a food to please the Gods."

—Ingrid Goff-Maidoff

Contrary to what most people believe, honey does not confer nutritional benefits and should not be considered a "health" food. Consisting of 80 percent fructose and glucose sugars and 18 percent water, honey contains the same calories pound for pound as sugar, but as it is sweeter you need less of it.

Honey varies according to the source of the nectar and method of production. Available in different colours from light (fireweed, clover, canola) to amber (sunflower) to dark (buckwheat, goldenrod), each has its own distinct taste.

Commercial brands of honey are often pasteurized and blended for uniform flavour: in the pasteurization process, honey is heated to 135F (57C) for 30 minutes to kill yeasts that can cause fermentation. This process also reduces the possibility of the honey forming crystals. Nutritionally, though, it's best to buy unpasteurized, unfiltered honey from a single flower source.

If Substituting One Cup of Sugar with Honey

For 1 cup (250 mL) sugar, substitute ¾ cup (180 mL) honey.

For every cup of sugar replaced, reduce the liquid in your recipe by ¼ cup (60 mL) to allow for the moisture in honey.

Add 3/8 tsp (2 mL) baking soda for every ¾ cup (180 mL) honey added.

Reduce the oven temperature by 25F (15C).

Organic Raw Cane Sugar

Processing sugar cane extracts juice from the cane, separates out the molasses and inorganic impurities, and bleaches and crystallizes the sugar by use of a centrifugal process. Brown sugar is not much better than white sugar, as it is made by just adding molasses to refined sugar. Organic raw cane sugar, which has not been subjected to heat and chemicals, and retains more molasses, is the healthiest option.

Molasses

When sugar-cane leaves are boiled to separate the sugar, this process creates a thick, dark syrup called molasses. The first boil results in the molasses with the highest sugar content and sweetest flavour. Blackstrap molasses—darker and less sweet— is the product of a second boiling.

Coconut Sugar

Light brown with the natural goodness of coconut water, coconut sugar (also called coconut sap sugar or evaporated coconut water) is made from the sap of the coconut tree.

Muscovado Sugar

Muscovado sugar is a natural, high-energy sweetener made from soaking sugar cane, then filtering and evaporating the water until the sugar crystallizes. No other refinement takes place, so it is the least processed of all cane sugars.

Maple Syrup

Maple syrup is the boiled-down sap of the sugar maple tree. Pure organic maple syrup is a natural unprocessed food with no removal of any nutrients. Raw-food enthusiasts often include maple syrup in their diet as an alternative source of sugar. Maple syrup has fewer calories than corn syrup and honey, averaging only 50 a tablespoon, and its nutritional value is far superior to honey and cane sugar.

Note: As with all natural unprocessed foods, check the best-before date and refrigerate after opening. Recently a friend of mine came down with a bad dose of food poisoning resulting from maple syrup that had mould growing in it!

Stevia

The South American herb *Stevia rebaudiana* provides a non-caloric sweetener. Only tiny amounts of the fresh or dried leaves are needed to provide a sweetening effect in recipes. Try adding a few dried leaves to hot herb teas and a few fresh leaves to summer iced teas for a sweetening effect.

Agave Syrup

The nectar produced by the agave plant is 75 percent sweeter than sugar. For the most nutritious and delicious product, look for certified-organic agave syrup that is dark in colour—a light colouring indicates it has been heavily filtered, which removes flavour. Choose agave syrup that has been naturally fermented using simple filtration techniques, not a brand that has been processed with heat or chemicals or any other synthetic material.

Hen egg vs. duck egg.

EGGS

The best eggs to eat are organic and free-range and from happy hens allowed to roam outdoors in fresh air, choosing what to eat from a natural pasture. You can identify an egg from a healthy hen because the shell is strong, the yolk golden-yellow, the flavour delicious.

How to Store

Eggs have a short storage life and should always be kept refrigerated. Freshness is paramount where eggs are concerned. If you are not sure about how fresh an egg is, perform a simple test by placing it in a bowl of cold water. If the egg sinks and lies flat, it is fresh. If it stands on end, it is not fresh. If it floats, it should not be eaten!

DAIRY

Dairy products include milk, cheese, butter and yogourt, all of which provide valuable amounts of protein, calcium, potassium, phosphorus and vitamins A, B_{12} and D. Dairy foods can be high in fat, so should be eaten in moderation.

Most milk and dairy products produced commercially today have been homogenized or pasteurized. Homogenization prevents the cream from separating, so the tiny fat molecules will be evenly dispersed throughout the milk. Pasteurization heats milk to a temperature high enough to kill bacteria, but also destroys enzymes and compromises nutritional integrity. Dairy products available in supermarkets today are nothing like the unpasteurized, unhomogenized milk of the past.

Raw unpasteurized milk is one of the best foods we can consume, but even though many people have raised their children on raw milk, it is generally illegal and not available commercially, because of the possibility of bacterial contamination. In many areas, raw milk can be purchased (illicitly!) directly from the dairy farmer, and in some cases the solution to restrictive laws has been to create cow-share programs, in which the farmer keeps and milks the cows, which are owned by the individuals who get to enjoy living milk. The good news is that it's not illegal to make some hard cheeses from unpasteurized milk, because the fermentation process eats up any bad bacteria, and at the same time consumes all the lactose. As a result, cheese made from raw milk is not only more digestible but also lactose-free.

Butter

The best butter available commercially comes from pasture-fed cows, even if it is pasteurized due to legal requirements. The majority of dairy cows today are raised in confinement on a diet of grain, particularly corn, because it is more cost efficient. Butter from cows grazing on pasture is richer in nutrients, because living grass is a better source of vitamins A and E as well as the antioxidant beta carotene than stored dried hay or standard dairy diets. Products from milk from pasture-fed cows have a higher content of healthier omega-3 fatty acids over the inflammation-causing omega-6 fatty acids.

THE A TO Z OF
CULINARY HERBS

RECIPES

Culinary lavender.

Instead of plying the aisles in a grocery store for miniature bottles of sauces and seasonings—a selection that always blows my mind and baffles my senses—why not enjoy the health benefits and taste sensations of homegrown herbs? The secret to a delicious meal is the flavour, and there's nothing tastier than seasonings made from plants you have growing in the garden.

In this section, I explore the myriad roles fresh and dried herbs can have in your diet, and you will also see these herbs appearing frequently in many of the seasonal recipes. In addition, I share the numerous ways I use herbs in the kitchen, and have included tasty recipes for seasonings that you can keep on hand. You may wish to refer to *The Zero-Mile Diet: A Year-Round Guide to Growing Organic Food* for more in-depth gardening information about growing herbs. I hope this chapter leaves you delighted and inspired to grow a garden full of wonderful herbal treasures for yourself.

Anise

The herb anise (*Pimpinella anisum*) is from the carrot family, Apiaceae. This plant is well known for aromatic seeds—aniseed—which look like fennel seeds and have the refreshing taste of licorice. Lightly roasted, they are delicious when chewed as a breath freshener after spicy meals. Aniseed quickly loses flavour, so is best stored in an airtight container.

Anise is primarily associated with cakes, biscuits and confectionery, as well as with rye bread. It is also used to flavour fish, poultry, soups and root-vegetable dishes. Anise's carminative properties aid digestion.

Anise will not produce ripe seeds without a long, hot summer, and the seeds are ready for gathering when they change colour from lime-green to grey-green. To harvest, cut the flower stems and hang them upside down in a dry place, collecting seeds as they fall onto paper below. TIP: Anise does not like to be pot grown or transplanted, so sow fresh seeds directly into warm soil.

Basil

Basil (*Ocimum basilicum*) is a tender, aromatic annual that comes in many flavours, from lemon to cinnamon to spicy Thai. Basil seeds require warmth for germination and plants need heat to thrive. To keep basil plants bushy, pinch out the growing tips to harvest. Fresh basil can be kept for a short time in plastic bags in the refrigerator.

Basil leaves are a treat in season, when they can be added to tomato dishes, tucked into paninis and sandwiches, and added to salads. They are a staple in Italian and Thai cooking. The leaves turn black when

Top: Dark opal basil makes beautiful purple herb vinegar.

Bottom: Lettuce leaf and Genovese basil are the best to grow for making pesto.

bruised and when heated or too cold, so handle them gently and preferably use them fresh and whole. If cooking with basil leaves, add to the recipe at the last moment, as prolonged cooking destroys their delicate flavour. Pesto is a basil sauce that enlivens many dishes—pasta, fish, omelettes and vegetables—as well as being a delicious spread on crackers. Make pesto when basil is readily available, and freeze it in ice cubes or containers for use throughout the year. See Garlic Scape Pesto (page 150).

Bay leaves should be dried before use. Just spread them out on a tray beside a sunny window to dry.

Bay

Bay (*Laurus nobilis*) is a slow-growing evergreen tree with glossy-green aromatic leaves. A tender perennial, it can be killed off by harsh weather, so is best grown in a pot and brought indoors for the winter. Bay is slow to root from tip cuttings, but it's worth having a backup plan if you want to be sure to have the fragrant leaves handy in the kitchen cupboard. I toss dried bay leaves into many dishes, removing them once the dish is cooked. They add considerable flavour to soups, sauces, curries, casseroles and plain steamed rice.

Bouquet Garni

You can introduce the subtle flavours of woody perennial herbs to homemade meals and soups by making bouquet garni—basically a bag of herbs that is added to soups and stews and removed before serving. Bay is an essential ingredient in bouquet garni.

6 sprigs parsley

1 bay leaf

2 tsp (10 mL) thyme

1 leek, the white part, chopped

2 garlic cloves

1 lovage leaf or a sprig of celery leaves

Optional: Rosemary, savory, sweet marjoram, Greek oregano, tarragon, peppercorns

Put all the above ingredients in a cheesecloth bag and tie up with cotton thread or string. Bouquet garni recipes usually include parsley, thyme and a bay leaf, but may also contain rosemary, savory, sweet marjoram, Greek oregano, tarragon and peppercorns.

Place the bouquet-garni bag into the recipe at the beginning of cooking and let it remain until the dish is done.

Remove from the recipe once it has cooled. Untie the bag and empty the herbs into the compost.

Makes 1 bag

Chervil

Chervil (*Anthriscus cerefolium*) is an annual in the carrot family, Apiaceae. It has fine lacy foliage, and is easy to grow in cool seasons in sun to part shade. Fresh chervil is among the delicate *fines herbes* added to many dishes. Use it as you would parsley for a wonderful addition to salads and sandwiches. Traditionally, it is preserved in white wine vinegar.

Crosnes with Chervil

Crosnes (*Stachys affinis*) are French rustic root vegetables, also known as Chinese artichokes or chorogi. The little worm-resembling tubers were brought to France from Japan around the nineteenth century and named after the Crosne area near Paris. In France the vegetables are considered gourmet and served at upscale restaurants. In Asia they are called *chorogi*, which means "longevity," because of their nutritional value. Rich in protein, they also contain betaine, which improves digestion. Eaten raw, they taste similar to water chestnuts, with a nutty flavour. Cooked, they have the texture of potato and taste like sunchokes.

2 lb (908 gr) crosnes
2 Tbsp (30 mL) coarse salt
1 Tbsp (15 mL) extra virgin olive oil
3 cloves garlic, minced
2 Tbsp (30 mL) salted butter
½ tsp (2.5 mL) sea salt
¼ tsp (1 mL) black pepper
2 Tbsp (30 mL) chervil, chopped
1 lemon, freshly squeezed

Crosnes are French rustic root vegetables, also known as Chinese artichokes or chorogi. They are so easy to grow that I offer a "beware" clause: they spread fast and multiply so rapidly that just a few plants will go a very long way!

Gently brush the crosnes, carefully removing any dirt. Place the coarse salt and crosnes in a towel; rub between your hands and then rinse the salt away. Place the crosnes in a steamer basket over a saucepan of water, and bring to the boil.

Lower the heat to a gentle simmer. Cover and cook for about 5 to 8 minutes.

Heat the olive oil over medium-high heat in a heavy-bottomed pan. Add the garlic and cook until golden. Add the butter and crosnes. Season with sea salt and pepper. Sauté for 2 to 3 minutes until tender.

Garnish with chervil and drizzle with lemon juice.

Bon appétit!

Makes 6 servings

* if using olive oil instead of butter

Chives

Chives (*Allium schoenoprasum*) are fast-multiplying perennial plants that grow in clumps up to 18 inches (45 cm) high with pretty edible blossoms. The easiest way to harvest chives is with a pair of sharp scissors, cutting off bunches and then snipping a handful into smaller pieces. Chives add a perfect hit of onion to egg, green and potato salads and salad dressings. They make an attractive garnish for soups and omelettes, or at the edge of the plate (especially if you leave the purple-pink blossoms attached).

Herb Butter GF

Use herb butter to liven up crackers, sandwiches, wraps, vegetables, omelettes, pasta and fish dishes. It's really useful stuff!

1 cup (250 mL) butter (unsalted preferred)
1 Tbsp (15 mL) Tomato Paste (see page 73)

Choose from one or more of these combinations to make veggie butter to suit your taste:

1 leek, finely minced
2 garlic cloves, minced
2 green onions, minced
2 tsp (10 mL) fresh dill
2 tsp (10 mL) fresh basil
2 tsp (10 mL) fresh Greek oregano
2 tsp (10 mL) fresh parsley or parcel
2 tsp (10 mL) fresh chives or garlic chives
2 tsp (10 mL) fresh chervil
2 tsp (10 mL) fresh fennel leaves

Place the butter and tomato paste in the bowl of a food processor. Add herbs of your choice and blend into a smooth consistency. Spoon the herb butter into glass storage dishes or ramekins, and keep in the fridge until use.

Makes 1 cup (250 mL)

Coriander

Coriander (*Coriandrum sativum*), also known as Chinese cilantro, is an annual herb grown for its pungent leaves, an essential ingredient in Mexican and Latin American cuisine. Coriander is best grown from a direct seeding, as seedlings don't transplant well. TIP: For continuous harvest, sow seeds every three to four weeks. Coriander overwinters in mild climates. Otherwise it needs protection under a cloche or inside a greenhouse. See Cilantro Chutney (page 240).

Dill

Dill (*Anethum graveolens*) provides leaves of distinctive flavour—dillweed—as well as seeds that are appreciated in many dishes. Dillweed is tasty combined with potato and egg or squash and cucumber dishes, cabbage greens, sauces, salads and dressings. It is added when curing wild salmon (gravlax) and as a traditional flavouring to borscht soup. Dill seeds are a valued ingredient in pickling recipes (and sometimes the flower is also added). And dill seeds are also traditionally used to aid digestion after meals.

The best time to harvest is just before flowering, when volatile oils are highest. Harvest the seeds once a majority on the head has matured, when they can be lightly threshed into a container. As dill seedlings hate disturbance, it's best to sow fresh seed directly into warm garden beds. In sunny weather and well-drained, sandy soil with low pH, dill can grow up to 3 ft. (1 m) and will reseed readily.

See Dilled Green Beans (page 80).

Fennel

Sweet fennel (*Foeniculum vulgare dulce*) is a tough perennial and easy to grow. The airy leaves

Sandy grabs a bunch of fresh dill.

and aromatic seeds are harvested from this plant, which should not be confused with Florence fennel or finocchio (*Foeniculum vulgare azoricum*). Florence fennel is grown for its swollen base, and eaten both raw and cooked. The delicate licorice flavour of either fennel blends well with fish, tomato sauce, salads and dressings, pasta dishes and omelettes.

Bronze fennel (*Foeniculum vulgare rubrum*) is better suited to being an ornamental edible, though leaves and seeds can also be harvested for culinary use. If you grow fennel, be aware that the plants have deep roots once established and self-seed readily! Chewing fennel seeds after meals helps digestion.

Fines Herbes Salées du Bas-du-Fleuve
(Fines Herbes from the Lower River)

Jacynthe Bouchard's family preserved fresh herbs from the garden this way. They were used to enhance winter soups, stews and other recipes. Choose herbs from the garden, such as parsley, chervil, chives, oregano, sweet marjoram, thyme or summer savory. Fresh vegetables can include leeks, carrots, celery leaves, green onions or bulb onions.

1 cup (250 mL) processed herbs and/or vegetables
¼ cup (60 mL) coarse salt

Using a food processor, finely chop the fresh herbs and/or vegetables together. (If using carrots, they should be grated first.) Toss the chopped herbs thoroughly with the salt.

Put into a sealed glass jar and store in the refrigerator.

Wait 3 days before using. The herbs will keep in the fridge for up to 6 months.

Makes just over 1 cup (250 mL)

Left: A collection of herbs to make Fines Herbes Salées du Bas-du-Fleuve.

French Sorrel

French sorrel (*Rumex acetosa*) is a lemony-tasting perennial that can be eaten raw in salads, blended into dressings, cooked lightly to add a tangy zest to soups or used in place of lemon juice. Rich in potassium and vitamins A, B_1 and C, sorrel once helped to ward off scurvy, an affliction brought on in earlier times by the North American winter diet. Many people confuse French sorrel with spinach because they look similar. When using sorrel raw, choose leaves that are less than 6 inches (15 cm) long, and save larger leaves for cooking.

Add finely shredded sorrel to tomato- or fish-based soups at the last minute to avoid diminishing flavour. Sorrel does not dry well, but you can lightly steam the leaves, press out the liquid and freeze in ice cubes for use in recipes throughout the year. In any recipe that calls for spinach, you may substitute one part sorrel to three parts spinach.

Sorrel Sauce VG* GF

This versatile sauce makes a fitting accompaniment to roasted root vegetables, steamed greens, hearty lentils or vegan burger patties.

4 large French sorrel leaves, washed

6 oz (170 gr) Greek yogourt

1 garlic clove, crushed

2 Tbsp (30 mL) extra virgin olive oil

1 tsp (5 mL) sea salt

½ tsp (2.5 mL) Dijon mustard

Put the above ingredients into the bowl of a food processor and whiz into a bright-green sauce.

* if using soy yogourt

Chill until needed.

Makes just over 1 cup (250 mL)

Garlic Chives

Garlic chives (*Allium tuberosum*) are similar to chives, but the glossy green leaves are broad and flat instead of being hollow. Although standard chives have a mild onion flavour, garlic chives are known for a garlicky taste that enhances stir-fries, stews, soups, stuffings, eggs and seafood.

Lemon Balm

Lemon balm (*Melissa officinalis*) not only self-seeds readily, but as a member of the mint family runs vegetatively, too. Many gardeners curse this plant because they have allowed it to get away. Easily grown, lemon balm thrives in well-drained soil in sunny or sheltered positions, and once established becomes drought tolerant. TIP: Cut plants back hard after flowering for a fresh flush of leaves, and to prevent the seeds from maturing.

It's reassuring to have plenty of fresh leaves for soothing lemony tea, or to add a hit of lemon to salads. Traditionally used to reduce stress, lemon balm is considered a calming remedy, and is often combined with other soothing herbs such as valerian, chamomile and hops.

Lemon Verbena

Lemon verbena (*Aloysia triphylla*) is a deciduous shrub with elongated green leaves infused with an intense lemon flavour. The tender perennial loses leaves at temperatures below freezing, but the wood is hardy to 14F (-10C). The secret to success is pruning back hard after winter and at each leaf harvest, which prevents the shrub from sprawling and becoming weak.

The plant should be placed in full sun for the oils to develop well. Lemon verbena grows rapidly in hot summers, enough for two harvests of leaves to be taken to add flavour to fish dishes, vegetable marinades, salad dressings, jams, sorbets and lemonade. It also is used to make a soothing herbal tea. See Raspberry Lemon Verbena Iced Tea (page 186).

Lovage

Lovage (*Levisticum officinale*) is a fast-growing herbaceous perennial that grows to 6 ft. (2 m) tall by early summer, and produces pungent leaves with an intense celery flavour wonderful for soup stock. One large leaf will do the trick! Cut plants down to the ground after the first flush of growth and another flush replaces it. Lovage prefers moist soil and part shade, but it is easy to grow from seed and not really fussy.

*Right: Lovage (*Levisticum officinale*) makes the best soup stocks.*

Vegetable Stock with Lovage

A good stock is simple to make, particularly when you have garden-fresh ingredients on hand—and the secret to any great soup is the stock!

4 carrots

4 onions

1 bunch celery, including the leafy tops

2 large potatoes

2 leeks

4 tomatoes

12–18 cups (3–4.5 L) cold water

1 bay leaf

1 lovage leaf

6 garlic cloves

2 Tbsp (30 mL) sea salt

2 tsp (10 mL) fresh-ground black pepper

Chop the vegetables coarsely and put into a heavy pot with the water and seasonings. Cover the pot and bring to the boil. Reduce the heat and simmer for 2 hours.

Strain the stock and compost the vegetables.

Cool and refrigerate until use.

Makes 12 cups (3 L)

Q What are good ingredients to add to a soup stock?

A Add the peelings, tops and bottoms of many vegetables (often the best part!), such as carrots, celeriac or celery leaves and stalks, leeks, onions, finocchio fennel, tomatoes, hot peppers, salsify, potatoes and garlic. Also add herbs such as lovage, sweet marjoram, Greek oregano, parsley, tarragon and thyme.

Q What ingredients should I resist from throwing into a soup stock?

A Some things are best to avoid, either because the flavour or colour is overpowering, or because they have an unpleasant effect on taste when left to simmer for a long time. Beetroots, and all the members of the cabbage family—cauliflower, broccoli, kale greens, etc.—fall into this category.

Sweet Marjoram

Sweet marjoram (*Origanum marjorana*) is related to oregano, but has its own distinctive fragrance that is treasured for many culinary purposes. Best grown in full sun to strengthen the aroma, it is recognized as an ingredient for bouquet garni and Herbes de Provence. Sweet marjoram complements any tomato dish, such as ratatouille.

It's also a potentially invasive low-growing groundcover, with small leaves and delicate flowers. Harvest leaves just before the flowers open and after the sun has dried the morning dew. The flavour improves when the herb is dried.

Mint

There are many strains of mint (*Mentha* spp.), some more hardy than others, and each with their own distinct flavour. Mints fall into spearmint varieties (larger leaves) or peppermint varieties (smaller leaves). The flavour ranges from fruity (grapefruit and pineapple) to savoury (black peppermint and ginger). All mints can be invasive if given the right conditions, so controlled growth is advised.

You can make delicious tea blends by combining different varieties of mint. Try steeping together fresh sprigs of chocolate and lavender mint, or ginger and apple mint, for a delightful summer tea. In winter enjoy the same using dried mint leaves.

To dry, harvest the mint on a sunny day, after the dew has dried, when the flavour is at its peak. Pick young fresh shoots about 6 inches (15 cm) long and tie them together in small bunches. To capture the essential oil, put mint leaves inside a paper bag, and hang the bag in a warm dark place with good air circulation. After a few days, the dried herbs should be ready to store in airtight jars in a dark place, which

Sweet marjoram is an ingredient for bouquet garni and Herbes de Provence.

There are many kinds of mint to try—just don't let them take over your garden!

prevents deterioration from light. TIP: Herbs lose flavour over time, so replenish annually.

See Tangy Mint Tzatziki (page 150) and Fresh Mint Tabouleh (page 159).

Greek Oregano

Origanum vulgare hirtum is the true Greek oregano, with flavour so intense it numbs the end of your tongue when eaten fresh. The way to tell if it's true is that the flowers are white and not purple. Oregano can be difficult to grow in areas of excessive winter rain, but will thrive in pots and planters, which can be brought inside for the winter months.

Greek oregano can be forced into renewed growth by shearing the plant back to within 2 inches (5 cm) of the ground, following the first flush of growth. This technique discourages flowering and encourages bushiness. When dry, store whole stems of the fragrant herb in glass jars in a dark cupboard. TIP: Leaving the leaves on the stem instead of stripping them off preserves more flavour. Greek oregano can be used for marinades, sauces or salads, pizza, soups and casseroles, or any tomato-based dish. Dried sprigs with garlic, coarse salt and olive oil make a great marinade for roast potatoes or vegetables.

Herb Marinated Olives `VG` `GF`

I know olives aren't "zero mile" where I live, but the herbs and the lemons are, and this recipe makes a wonderful appetizer for olive lovers!

8 oz (225 gr) black olives

8 oz (225 gr) green olives

4 Tbsp (60 mL) extra virgin olive oil

3 small sprigs each of fresh thyme, rosemary and Greek oregano

3 bay leaves, dried

1 large garlic clove, thinly sliced

2 lemons, quartered

Toss all the ingredients together. Leave to marinate in the refrigerator until use.

Makes 2 cups (475 mL)

Parcel

Parcel (*Apium graveolens*) is one of my top-10 kitchen herbs because it combines the best of parsley and celery in a winter-hardy plant. I use parcel a lot, so sow it in rows that are easy to harvest with scissors as cut-and-come-again greens. Like parsley, parcel is a biennial, so it self-seeds every second year, which means you will always have more of this wonderful herb.

Parsley

Parsley (*Petroselinum hortense*) is so versatile that it's probably the most commonly used herb in the kitchen. It's up to you whether you prefer the dense moss-curled, delicate lacy-leaved or convenient flat-leaved strains. Parsley is perfect for soups and salads, green smoothies, pasta dishes, potato dishes, casseroles and any tomato-based dish.

Parsley is a biennial—which means it produces seed in the second year of growth. Resist the temptation to cut the flower heads off, and allow the seeds to mature and drop (a slow process), so that you always have a patch of parsley in your garden.

Parcel combines the best of celery and parsley in one winter-hardy plant.

Rosemary

Rosemary (*Rosmarinus officinalis*) means "dew of the sea" and is most closely associated with traditional Mediterranean cuisine. I think gardeners underestimate rosemary as a worthwhile ornamental shrub. It's a tender perennial evergreen with the prettiest sky-blue flowers in spring. It survives all but the worst winters, so I now grow plants in ceramic pots, and bring them in for the winter. Rosemary is easily propagated from tip cuttings, and I like having a few extras around.

Rosemary has glossy, dark-green needles with intense aromatic flavour, which can be used both fresh and dried, and complement a wide variety of foods. The influence is strong so you don't need much to affect the flavour. Rosemary can be harvested year-round, an ideal time being just after flowering, when a good cutting back will strengthen and tidy up the shrub. You can either strip needles off the stem after drying, or use whole sprigs to flavour food, removing them after cooking.

HOW TO USE ROSEMARY

- Flavour olive oil with fresh sprigs.
- Add a kick to vegetable marinades.
- Burn sprigs on the barbecue to add a woody flavour to food being grilled.
- Throw sprigs into a garlic roaster with cloves of garlic.
- Make rosemary-flavoured vinegar.
- Roast with onions for a tasty effect.
- Add to roast potatoes.
- Add leaves to breads such as focaccia.
- Combine with sage and thyme for a savoury stuffing.

Sage

Culinary sage (*Salvia officinalis*) is a drought-tolerant, grey-leaved shrub that thrives in full sun and well-drained soil. 'Holt's Mammoth' is one of my favourite varieties, because this broadleaf perennial is particularly ornamental with its upright violet-blue flower spikes in spring.

It's best to dry sage leaves slowly to retain their powerful aroma, and to remember that a little sage goes a long way. Culinary sage goes well with bean dishes, cheese, lentils and vegan pâté, and as an ingredient in stuffing and nut loaf. A tea infusion of the leaves will provide soothing relief for a sore throat or loss of voice.

Savory

Summer savory (*Satureja hortensis*) is an aromatic bushy annual with a distinct yet delicate piquancy that does not overpower other foods. Savory dries well and once dried is an integral part of Herbes de Provence and bouquet garni. These blends of Mediterranean herbs bring out the best in casseroles, vegetable dishes and pizza. Savory is especially well known for its complementary effect on green beans. It also improves egg dishes. The tender leaves can be added fresh to salads or used as a garnish. A useful way to preserve its delicate flavour is to bottle the herb at the height of its season in white wine vinegar.

Winter savory (*Satureja montana*) is a hardy, semi-evergreen compact bush, with leaves of pronounced flavour. The aromatic leaves benefit slow-cooked dishes such as soups and stews, and are often added to water when cooking dried beans, lentils and peas. Savory also combines well with other herbs in stuffings.

Sweet Cicely

Sweet cicely (*Myrrhis odorata*) has ferny leaves that are anise-flavoured. Combined with rhubarb, sweet cicely allows you to cut the amount of sugar used in half. The whole plant—leaves, seeds and roots—is edible. The root has a sweet anise taste, easily yielding

Umbels of tiny white flowers appear on Sweet Cicely in May and June, attracting lots of beneficial insects to the garden.

these properties to water or diluted alcohol. Chewing on the young green seed pods of sweet cicely is a great breath freshener.

Tarragon

If you are going to grow tarragon, ensure it is French tarragon (*Artemisia dracunculus* var. *sativa*) and not Russian tarragon, which many consider to possess no culinary virtue. Russian tarragon is grown from seed; French tarragon seed is sterile and so the plant is not so readily available. A short-lived tender perennial, French tarragon spreads into clumps but needs to be renewed often. My advice? If you want this desirable herb in your garden, make divisions frequently and spread them throughout the garden.

One of the fines herbes of French cooking, along with parsley, chives and chervil, tarragon leaves can be used fresh or dried. The unique, sweet anise flavour is particularly suited to fish, pasta, vinaigrettes, and artichoke, asparagus and egg dishes. Tarragon also adds exquisite flavour to herbal vinegar.

Thyme

Thyme (*Thymus vulgaris*) is a woody sub-shrub that once established is drought tolerant and easy to grow. It has small grey-green aromatic leaves, and to maintain its shape is best pruned back hard after flowering. The delicate flowers of all varieties of thyme are highly attractive to bees (and thyme-infused honey is a gourmet treat).

Culinary thyme should not be confused with the many other species of thyme. Creeping thyme and silver thyme are commonly grown as decorative groundcovers but are not useful in the kitchen. Lemon thyme and common thyme are best for eating. The leaves retain flavour well when dried, and for this reason thyme is a key ingredient in bouquet garni and Herbes de Provence.

Thyme is wonderful roasted with vegetables and thrown into the garlic roaster with garlic cloves. It's a key ingredient in savoury stuffings, and goes well in soups and stews, and with any tomato, lentil or bean dish. Lemon thyme with its pronounced lemon fragrance is particularly good with fish dishes. As a woody herb, thyme releases its aroma slowly, so it is usually added earlier on in cooking.

Herbal Vegetable Salt `VG` `GF`

For those who want to avoid adding salt to food, this homemade alternative is perfect.

- 1 cup (250 mL) dried chard leaves
- 1 cup (250 mL) dried kale leaves
- ½ cup (125 mL) dried thyme
- ½ cup (125 mL) dried Greek oregano
- 3 Tbsp (45 mL) dried seaweed
- 1 Tbsp (15 mL) dried cayenne pepper flakes

Put all the ingredients into a food processor and blend into a fine mixture on high speed for 30 seconds, without grinding to the powder stage.

Store in a sealed container.

Makes 3 cups (700 mL)

Gourmet Herbal Vegetable Salt

To the above recipe add:

- 1 cup (250 mL) dried tomatoes, minced
- 1 cup (250 mL) dried sweet peppers, minced
- 1 cup (250 mL) dried leeks, onions or carrots, finely chopped (optional)

HERBAL TEAS

`VG` `GF`

How to Prepare Herbs

INFUSION

An infusion is the simplest way to make a tea, using herbs either fresh or dried. Infusions are best for the leaves, flowers, petals and green stems of herbs. For the harder and woodier bark, seeds and roots, it's best to dry and powder them first for a more potent infusion and to release their volatile oils. A mortar and pestle work well for this purpose, or you can use a rolling pin.

When making an infusion, remember these basic rules:

1 part dried herb = 3 parts fresh herb
1 oz (28 gr) of dried herb to 2 cups (475 mL) of boiling water

First, warm a teapot, and add 1 tsp (5 mL) dried herb for each cup (250 mL) of water. Replace the lid (which should be tight-fitting to avoid the escape of volatile oils through evaporation). Leave to steep for 10 to 15 minutes. Infusions may be drunk hot or cold. They can also be sweetened with honey, stevia, anise or raw cane sugar. It is best to prepare a fresh infusion for each use, but teas can also be stored in the refrigerator to prolong availability.

GOOD TEA HERBS

- Anise Hyssop
- Lemon Verbena
- Bee Balm
- Mint
- Calendula
- Rosemary
- Chamomile
- Sage
- Lavender
- Scented Geraniums
- Lemon Balm
- Tulsi (Sacred Basil)

Decoction

For harder roots, rhizomes, wood, bark, nuts and seeds, more heat is needed to break down cell walls. In this case it's best to make a decoction, when the herbs are boiled in water. Dried herbs should be powdered, or cut into smaller pieces. TIP: Never use aluminum pots. Instead, choose glass, ceramic, earthenware or enamelled metal pots.

For each 1 cup (250 mL), put 1 tsp (5 mL) dried herb or 1 Tbsp (15 mL) fresh into 1 cup (250 mL) water. Bring to the boil and simmer covered for 10 to 15 minutes. Strain and serve hot.

Chamomile flowers are fast to dry on a wire-mesh screen.

HERBAL VINEGARS

VG GF

Herbal vinegars are easy to prepare. You can use red wine vinegar, white wine vinegar, rice vinegar or apple cider vinegar. Generally the stronger-flavoured herbs go best with the stronger-flavoured vinegars.

Rule of Thumb

**1 cup (250 mL) loosely packed herbs:
2 cups (475 mL) vinegar**

Wash the herbs. Bruise them slightly with a wooden spoon to release their aroma, then stuff them into a sterilized glass jar and cover with vinegar. Put the lid on the jar and leave to infuse in a sunny window or a warm place for 3 to 4 weeks, depending on how strong you want the herbal vinegar to taste. Shake weekly.

Strain through a cheesecloth-lined sieve to filter.

Fill a clean, sterilized glass bottle with the vinegar and seal with a cork.

Store in a cool, dark place.

Choose from one or a combination of the following:
Herbs: Rosemary, thyme, savory, dill, basil, chervil, tarragon, sweet marjoram, oregano or bay leaf
Flowers: Calendula petals or lavender flowers
Vegetables: Garlic cloves, shallots or chili peppers
Spices: Peppercorns or mustard seeds
Fruit: Raspberries, blackberries, tayberries or lemon rind

You can produce purple vinegar by using opal basil in white vinegar. Make fruity vinegar by adding raspberries or blackberries to any vinegar.

EAT YOUR FLOWERS!

Give an elegant touch to recipes by adding edible flowers. Sprinkle them into vegetable and fruit salads, and use them to decorate dishes. Make celebratory desserts and cakes look really special with edible flower art.

When selecting flowers for culinary purposes, be certain you know what part of the plant is edible and only choose flowers that are pesticide-free. Flowers are fragile and should be used soon after harvest for best effect.

The Edible Flower Garden

- Alliums (onion family)—eat and enjoy all parts.
- Anise hyssop has licorice-flavoured flower spikes.
- Arugula flowers have a nutty, spicy flavour.
- Bachelor's button (cornflower) provides edible flowers in pink, purple, white or blue.
- Bee balm's red flowers are edible.
- Broccoli's pale-yellow florets are a delicate garnish with a fresh, crisp flavour.
- Borage provides bright-blue petals with a refreshing cucumber taste.
- Calendula's orange petals pretty up all dishes.
- Chives' purple blossoms have an oniony taste.

'Rainbow loveliness' dianthus have sweet-tasting petals.

- Carnations (*Dianthus* spp.) serve up sweet-tasting petals.
- Chamomile flowers make a soothing tea.
- Chervil's white flowers have an anise flavour.
- Chicory's pale-blue petals and buds are edible.
- Cilantro's delicate white flowers add flavour similar to cilantro itself.
- Clover has licorice-flavoured blossoms.
- Day lily's large flowers are edible.
- Dill's yellow flowers are edible.
- Jasmine's flowers are traditionally used to flavour teas.
- Lavender has fragrant purple flowers that can be added to recipes, fresh or dried.
- 'Lemon' and 'Tangerine Gems' marigolds are edible.
- Lilac's purple or white blossoms have a lemony flavour.
- Mustard's bright-yellow flowers add a hint of spiciness.
- Nasturtium provides peppery flowers and crisp edible leaves.
- Pansies—the entire flower is edible.
- Garden peas have edible flowers.
- Pineapple sage's red flowers are sweet.
- Primrose's flowers have a delicate fragrance.
- Rosemary's pink or blue blossoms have a rosemary flavour.
- Roses—the petals are sweet tasting, but eat only the petals!
- Squash flowers are delicious, but remove the stamens before eating.
- Shungiku's flower petals are edible.
- Sunflower's petals can be used as a garnish.
- Violets have delicate edible flowers in pink or blue.
- Violas provide delicate and sweet-tasting pretty flowers.

Lavender

To preserve lavender, cut 6-inch (15-cm) long stems when the flowers are first showing colour. Gather into small bunches and hang in a warm shady place to dry.

Laveroons (Lavender Macaroons) GF

These fragrant and chewy treats are perfect with a cup of tea or as dessert following a meal. Thanks to Lynda Dowling for her lavender inspiration for this recipe.

1 cup (250 mL) finely ground almonds

¾ cup (180 mL) icing sugar

½ cup (125 mL) berry sugar

1 tsp (5 mL) dried lavender flowers, stripped off stalks

½ cup (125 mL) egg whites, room temperature (from 3–4 large eggs)

Pinch salt

½ tsp (2.5 mL) pure almond extract

Preheat oven to 350F (175C) and line two baking trays with parchment paper.

Pass the ground almonds and icing sugar together through a fine sieve to remove lumps and large almond pieces. Place ¼ cup (60 mL) berry sugar and the lavender into a spice grinder or food processor and pulse until the lavender and sugar are finely powdered. Stir lavender sugar into almond sugar mixture and set aside.

In a clean bowl using electric beaters (or a stand-mixer), beat the egg whites with a pinch of salt until they are foamy. Gradually add the remaining ¼ cup (60 mL) berry sugar, beating until smooth and creamy with stiff peaks.

Using a spatula, gently fold the almond extract and almond/lavender/sugar mixture into the egg whites, until no more dry ingredients can be seen. Try not to over mix.

Using a tablespoon or piping bag, evenly place 20 mounds of batter onto the cookie sheet allowing room for spreading as they bake. (For 40 smaller cookies, use a teaspoon.) Allow cookies to sit on the counter for about 10 minutes, until they begin to lose their glossy appearance—this will help to retain their shape during baking and create a crispy crust with a moist, chewy interior.

Leave the oven door very slightly ajar to allow steam to escape and bake for 15 to 20 minutes

For a decadent presentation, sandwich a layer of homemade blueberry preserves between two laveroons.

in the centre of the oven until the bottom of the laveroons are lightly golden.

Remove the baking sheet from the oven and allow to cool slightly. Then gently peel the parchment paper away from the laveroons and put them on a wire rack to fully cool. Store in an airtight tin.

Makes 20 large or 40 small cookies

PRESERVING THE HARVEST

RECIPES

Storing Garden Produce

COOL AND DRY STORAGE

Onions

Store at temperatures from 32 to 50F (0 to 10C) and 60 to 70 percent relative humidity.

Choose late-maturing onion varieties with thin necks for long-term storage. Harvest onions on a dry day, once the tops droop over, and allow them to cure in the sun for several days. Trim the tops to about 1 inch (2.5 cm), and continue to cure for another 2 to 3 weeks in a dry, shady location. Once cured, they can be stored in mesh bags or other breathable containers for several months.

Garlic

Store at temperatures from 32 to 50F (0 to 10C) and 50 percent relative humidity.

Garlic should be harvested when about two-thirds of the leaves have turned yellow. Allow garlic to cure in a dry, well-ventilated place for 2 to 4 weeks. Trim the roots, removing any soil attached. Trim the top, leaving about 1 inch (2.5 cm), and store in paper or mesh bags.

COLD AND MOIST STORAGE

Beets, Carrots, Parsnips, Turnips and Rutabagas

Store at temperatures from 32 to 40F (0 to 4C) and 80 to 95 percent relative humidity in a refrigerator, cooler or root cellar.

Beets, carrots, parsnips, turnips and rutabagas prefer a higher humidity range from 80 to 95 percent. Harvest them in the fall, trim their tops to within ½ inch (1 cm) and rinse them (without scrubbing). Let them dry, then store them in plastic bags with perforated holes to help keep in the moisture while maintaining airflow.

Potatoes

Store at temperatures from 32 to 40F (0 to 4C) and 80 to 90 percent relative humidity in a refrigerator, cooler or root cellar.

Potatoes can also be stored with beets, carrots, parsnips, turnips and rutabagas, but they prefer slightly lower humidity levels from 80 to 90 percent. Harvest after the vines have died and dried up, taking care not to bruise the crop. Do not wash or scrub the potatoes, but any soil should be gently brushed from the tubers. They need to be cured for 1 to 2 weeks in a warm, moist and dark location at 60 to 75F (15 to 25C) and should then store for four months or longer.

WARM AND DRY STORAGE

Pumpkins and Winter Squash

After harvest, cure at temperatures from 80 to 85F (27 to 29C) for about 2 weeks before moving to long-term storage. Store at temperatures from 50 to 60F (10 to 15C) and 60 to 75 percent relative humidity.

Pumpkins and winter squash can cure together, though pumpkins prefer slightly higher humidity. When the fruits are fully mature and the skin has hardened (cannot be punctured by a fingernail) they are ready to be harvested. Harvest before hard frosts hit, as frost damage shortens shelf life. Leave the stem intact when harvesting, because removing the stem leaves an open wound susceptible to spoilage. Pumpkins and squash will store best if arranged in a single layer spaced about 1 inch (2.5 cm) apart.

Acorn Squash

Store at temperatures from 45 to 50F (7 to 10C) and 60 to 75 percent relative humidity.

When fully mature, acorn squash develops an orange spot where the fruit has been in contact with the ground. Acorn squash should not be cured and requires lower storage temps of about 45 to 50F (7 to 10C) to maintain good flavour and texture.

FREEZING FRUITS AND VEGETABLES

Rules for Freezing Quality Food

- Select only peak-quality, blemish-free fruits and vegetables.
- Maintain a temperature of 0F (-18C) or less in the freezer to prevent deterioration of food quality. Extremely cold temperatures retard the growth of micro-organisms, as well as slow down the activity of food-spoiling enzymes.
- Freeze smaller loads of food fast to keep the ice crystals small. The maximum amount that should be frozen at once is about 2 to 3 lb (1 to 1.5 kg) of food for each cubic foot of freezer space.
- Freeze fruits and vegetables on trays in single layers—that's the best way. When they are frozen, pack the individual pieces into containers or freezer bags. This way you only use as much as you need when cooking, rather than having to use a single solid block of frozen food.
- Choose storage containers with straight sides. They stack better so that you can get more in the freezer.
- Leave headspace for expansion in the container, so it does not break or burst the seal. Too much space allows air in, which spoils food quality.
- When using freezer bags, press all the air out of the bag before sealing.
- Defrost the freezer when the ice has built up to ½-inch (1-cm) thickness on the sides. Thick ice makes freezers work hard to maintain 0F (-18C).
- Use permanent felt-tip pens to label containers or bags.
- Rotate freezer food, so there is a steady turnover of using the oldest food first.

Freezing Fruits

Apples, berries, cherries, peaches, plums and rhubarb all freeze well.

The maximum storage time for best-quality home-frozen fruit is 12 months.

TIP: Prevent apples, apricots, cherries, peaches and plums from browning oxidation by dipping them into ¼ cup (60 mL) lemon juice mixed with 4 cups (1 L) water.

Freezing Vegetables

Blanched asparagus, beans, broccoli, carrots, cauliflower, peas and summer squash, as well as cooked pumpkin, salsa, stewed tomatoes and sautéed mushrooms, all freeze well. The maximum storage time for best-quality home-frozen vegetables is 8 months.

Tomato Paste VG GF

Making your own tomato paste is the perfect way to use up bumper crops of large meaty tomatoes, and there's nothing to it! However, you will need a food mill (see page 32) for the job.

5 lb (2.3 kg) tomatoes, chopped coarsely

Fill a large stainless-steel pot with the chopped tomatoes. Bring to a boil, reduce the heat and allow the water to evaporate by slowly cooking over low heat uncovered for 3 to 4 hours, stirring occasionally to prevent sticking.

Allow to cool. Put everything in the pot through a food mill to remove the skins and produce a luscious thick paste of smooth consistency. Fill 1-cup (250-mL) plastic tubs with the tomato paste, label and freeze. Use in sauces, casseroles and for pizza and pasta dishes.

Makes 6 cups (1.5 L)

Tomatillo Salsa VG GF

You can make this piquant salsa using either green or purple tomatillos, and it's dynamite as a dip with chips or as an accompaniment to Bean and Cheese Burritos (page 230). If you prefer it less piquant, leave out the jalapeño pepper or replace it with a sweet pepper.

2 cups (475 mL) tomatillos, husks removed and halved

1 jalapeno pepper, halved and de-seeded

½ cup (125 mL) cilantro leaves, chopped

1 small onion, chopped

2 garlic cloves, minced

1 Tbsp (15 mL) fresh lime juice

About 1 tsp (5 mL) sea salt

Roast the husked tomatillos and pepper by placing them cut side down on a foil-lined baking sheet. Roast them under a grill for about 5 to 7 minutes, until the skin is lightly blackened.

Place the roasted tomatillos and pepper with the cilantro, onion, garlic and lime juice in a food processor. Pulse until finely chopped.

Adjust salt to taste. Refrigerate or freeze in small tubs.

Makes 2 cups (475 mL)

Blanching

Blanching is done in boiling water or by steaming, and destroys the enzymes that age vegetables in storage. In general, it takes no longer than three minutes to blanch vegetables, which must immediately be plunged into a cooling bath of water containing ice cubes, then drained and patted dry, before freezing.

Freezing Corn on the Cob

There's nothing more summery than sinking your teeth into the first cob of summer corn—the fresher, the sweeter. If you can't grow your own, go to your local farm the day they pick the corn fresh from the field. There are good savings to be had buying a "baker's dozen" (13 cobs for the price of 12); even better by buying a burlap sack of 6 dozen. Freeze the

Right: Corn can be frozen in the inner husk.

corn right away at the peak of flavour, and enjoy the taste of summer all winter long. TIP: Late-season corn freezes best, so ask for these varieties.

Contrary to what some books say, I've discovered that you don't need to blanch corn before freezing it—saving a lot of work. I simply whack the stalk off using a cleaver and strip off the outer husk, leaving the inner wrappers on. I freeze cobs of corn in recycled plastic buckets from the local deli.

When it comes time to eat the corn, rinse still-frozen cobs under warm water to remove the inner wrappers, and throw the cob into a pot of boiling water for exactly 10 minutes. This way, the eating quality is as good as the day the corn was harvested. For corn kernels, slice them off the cob while still frozen, using a serrated knife, and toss the kernels directly into the recipe.

FOOD DEHYDRATION

With a food dehydrator, you can capture the flavour and nutritive value of fruits, vegetables and herbs at their peak. Dehydration removes the natural water content of food by 80 to 90 percent, which inactivates the growth of bacteria, moulds, yeast and other spoilage organisms.

The first time I dried mushrooms they quickly turned into shrivelled pieces of "rubber." After referring to the dehydrator booklet for advice, I discovered that it is best to dry mushrooms at a lower temperature to start with, then finish at a higher heat. When you have three pounds of freshly harvested chanterelles at hand, it's good to know these things! In general, dried fruits will feel leathery and pliable; dried vegetables, brittle and tough.

The first dehydrator I bought had a motor with only 500 watts of power; the price may have been right at the time of purchase, but I paid the higher cost with mouldy tomatoes, mushrooms and fruit. My second dehydrator had twice as much drying power, and I lost no more dried food to mould. It takes a while to discover the individual drying requirements of different fruits and vegetables, and to get a sense of how fast or slowly to dry food, how thick or thin to make it, what temperature to dry it at and when to stop dehydrating for best results in flavour and texture. Here's a general guide based on what I have learned over the years:

Guide to Drying Times

FRUITS

Apples: 4–10 hours
Apricots: 8–16 hours
Blueberries: 10–18 hours
Cherries: 18–26 hours
Figs: 8–15 hours
Grapes: 10–36 hours
Peaches: 6–16 hours
Pears: 6–16 hours
Plums: 8–16 hours
Rhubarb: 6–14 hours
Strawberries: 6–12 hours

VEGETABLES

Carrots: 6–12 hours
Broccoli: 4–10 hours
Beans: 6–12 hours
Celery: 3–10 hours
Corn: 6–12 hours
Garlic: 6–12 hours
Mushrooms: 4–10 hours
Onions: 6–12 hours
Peppers: 3–20 hours
Tomatoes: 6–12 hours

HERBS

Basil, dill, marjoram, mint, oregano, parsley, rosemary, sage, tarragon and thyme should be dried at temperatures not exceeding 90–100F (32–38C). These garden herbs take from 45 minutes to 2½ hours to dry.

TIP: To preserve aroma, do not powder the dried leaves until ready to use.

Dried fruit is a treat for snacking and great for compotes.

Drying Temperatures

Fruits, fruit leathers and vegetables: 130–140F (55–60C)
Nuts and seeds: 90–100F (32–38C)
Herbs and spices: 90–100F (32–38C)

Tips for Dehydration of Fruits and Vegetables

- Select your harvest at the peak of freshness and flavour.
- Remove any bruised or damaged parts.
- Move through the slicing and chopping process swiftly to save valuable nutrients.
- Try to cut pieces of even thickness to keep the drying time consistent.
- When loading trays, do not overcrowd or overlap the food.
- If fruit browns on exposure to oxygen, toss the fruit in the fresh-squeezed juice of a lemon diluted with 2 cups (475 mL) of water. Apple and pear slices taste good with a hit of lemon and certainly look more appetizing.
- Keep records of what works best, as it varies from place to place according to humidity and climate.
- Know that some pieces dry faster than others. Toward the end of drying, check for and remove these pieces before they become over-dried.
- Check that vegetables are crisp, tough and brittle when properly dried.
- Store food immediately after drying to prevent moisture absorption.
- Store dehydrated food in airtight, moisture-proof containers. Glass jars stored in a dark cupboard work well.
- Wrap fruit leathers in plastic wrap and store them in airtight, moisture-proof containers.
- Label containers with the date of dehydration so that you can rotate stored foods efficiently.
- Store in a dark, cool, dry place. The temperature should be no higher than 60F (15C) to preserve the best quality and nutritive value of dehydrated foods.

Fruit Compotes

My favourite way to get healthy servings of orchard fruit in winter is by starting the day with some fruit compote—alone or combined with yogourt and granola, or on top of steaming oatmeal. I custom-blend compotes with different ingredients, but mine always have my own home-dried raisins in them! Over the winter months, we use our dehydrated fruit in many different ways—for snacks and hiking treats, and for adding to cookies, desserts or granola.

It's as easy as selecting a fruit mix in the evening and pouring boiling water over it to just cover.

The secret is to leave the fruit to rehydrate at room temperature for a few hours without putting a lid on the bowl. The longer the compote sits, the better the syrup becomes. TIP: Add a cinnamon stick and/or a slice of lemon during soaking to make the syrup even tastier.

You can soak the fruit in liquids other than water—such as fruit or vegetable juices—but it is best to hold back on adding seasonings such as sugar until right before eating, because they disrupt the rehydration process. Most fruits and vegetables rehydrate to 80 percent of their fresh condition.

HOME CANNING

The air we breathe, the water we drink and the soil in which we grow food contain bacteria, yeasts and moulds. These micro-organisms, together with enzymes, cause food to spoil as it ages, making it unpalatable and offensive. Moulds and yeasts naturally present in foods can produce mycotoxins that are harmful for us to eat. Fortunately, the acids in food prevent these bacteria from growing.

Moulds and yeasts are destroyed at temperatures from 140F to 190F (60C to 88C), so an effective way to prevent food spoilage is to expose food to heat, at the same time hermetically sealing it in glass jars. Enzymes that cause food to change flavour, colour and texture are also destroyed by temperatures higher than 140F (60C).

High-Acid Foods

High-acid foods are fruits, tomatoes, pickles, chutneys, jams and jellies. A boiling-water canner can be used for processing high-acid foods to 212F (100C), which destroys moulds and yeasts without compromising the quality of the product. If not correctly processed, deadly *Clostridium botulinum* (botulism) spores can grow in airtight jars, or in jars where lids have not sealed properly and there is leakage. For this reason, it's always advisable to check seals before consuming foods preserved by canning methods.

High-acid foods, such as jams, can be processed in a boiling water bath.

Low-Acid Foods

Low-acid foods are vegetables, meats, poultry, fish, soups and stews.

To avoid contamination of low-acid foods with deadly botulism bacteria, it is recommended these foods be processed using a pressure canner, which raises the temperature of the food to 240F (115C) to destroy spores of the bacteria. (I usually freeze garden vegetables—I don't like hissing pressure canners, so I don't own one!)

All the equipment you need to can peaches in a light honey syrup: canner with lid and rack, Mason jar, funnel, ladle, tongs, metal rings, snap lids and oven mitts.

Light Honey Syrup

I avoid losing the natural flavour of canned fruits by using a light honey syrup instead of sugar. The syrup accentuates the natural flavour without excess sweetness.

1 cup (250 mL) light honey

3 cups (700 mL) hot water

Simply blend the honey and hot water in a heat-proof bowl until the honey has dissolved. Then pour the hot syrup over the fruit in the canning jar before sealing and processing.

Fills four 1-quart (1-L) jars

How to Process High-Acid Foods

1. Wash Mason jars with hot, soapy water and rinse.
2. Fill a canner or large pot with water and heat it to boiling.
3. Using tongs, completely immerse the empty jars in the boiling water.
4. Allow the water to simmer at 180F (82C), leaving the jars immersed until ready for use.
5. Place the lids and metal rings in a small saucepan of water heated to 180F (82C), but do not allow the water to boil. Leave the lids and rings in the hot water until ready for use. TIP: Do not use recycled lids if the rubber seal has already been set.
6. Ladle hot food (hot pack) into the hot jars to prevent cracking from a sudden temperature change. (TIP: Use a wide-mouth funnel).
7. Leave ¼ inch (5 mm) of headspace for jams and jellies.
8. Leave ½ inch (1 cm) of headspace for fruit, pickles, tomatoes, chutney and relishes.
9. Using a sterilized, non-metallic utensil, remove any air bubbles in the jar and readjust the headspace if necessary.
10. If the jar rim is sticky, wipe it with a clean wet cloth.
11. Centre the snap lid on the jar, and twist the metal ring securely over it, but do not over-tighten.
12. Place the filled jars on the rack of a canner; when full, use oven mitts to lower the rack gently into the canner bath, three-quarters full of boiling water, so that the water covers the jars by at least 1 inch (2.5 cm).
13. Put the lid on the canner and bring the water back to a rolling boil.
14. Process for the time recommended by the recipe.
15. Turn off the heat and remove the canner lid. When the boiling water becomes still (approximately 5 minutes), carefully pull the rack up out of the canner by its handles, without tipping the jars, and place it on a heat-proof surface.
16. Using tongs, space the jars on a heat-proof surface (I use wooden bread boards), and leave them to cool upright, without adjusting the metal rings.
17. After cooling, check that all the lids are sealed. Sealed lids curve inward and do not move when tested. Jars that have not sealed can be refrigerated and consumed within 1 to 2 weeks.
18. Remove the metal rings if desired, and wipe the jars clean if sticky.
19. Label with type of food and date, and store in a cool, dark place.
20. Keep food processed in this way for up to 12 months.

PICKLING SALT

Formulated specifically for pickling and preserving, pickling salt is pure and fine-grained to ensure it dissolves easily and distributes evenly throughout the brine, providing the salinity required to make pickled foods safe to store and eat. Pickling salt can be replaced with kosher salt or table salt, though they may not perform as well. Iodized salt turns pickled foods dark, which makes them unappealing, and the anti-caking agents used in most salts will cloud the brine, which is also unsightly.

Substitute asparagus for beans in the Dilled Green Beans recipe (page 80) for a delicious way to store the spring crop.

Pickled Garlic

You'll be amazed how sweet garlic tastes once it has been pickled.

½ tsp (2.5 mL) mustard seeds

½ tsp (2.5 mL) celery seeds

2 cups (475 mL) white wine vinegar or apple cider vinegar

²/₃ cup (160 mL) granulated sugar

8 oz (225 gr) whole garlic cloves, peeled

1 large red pepper, seeded and thinly sliced

Place the mustard and celery seed in a cheesecloth bag, tied up with cotton string.

Put the vinegar and sugar in a saucepan, and bring to the boil for 5 minutes on medium-high heat, stirring until the sugar dissolves. Add the garlic cloves and the red pepper slices. Return to the boil, and boil for another 5 minutes. Discard the cheesecloth bag.

Fill a hot sterilized 1-pint (475-mL) Mason jar with the garlic and red peppers to within 1 inch

(2.5 cm) from the top. Fill the jar with the hot brine to within ¼ inch (5 mm) of the top. Wipe the rim of the jar clean, place the lid on top and fasten tight with the metal ring. Follow the steps in How to Process High-Acid Foods (see page 78) and process in a boiling-water canner for 10 minutes. Let stand several weeks in a cool, dark place before consuming.

Makes three 1-pint (475-L) jars

Dilled Green Beans

Seriously good crunchy beans!

3 lb (1.35 kg) whole green beans

6 garlic cloves, whole

6 cayenne peppers dried, or 1½ tsp (7.5 mL) cayenne pepper

6 heads of fresh dill or 2 Tbsp (30 mL) dill seeds

6 tsp (30 mL) peppercorns

3¼ cups (760 mL) vinegar

3¼ cups (760 mL) water

6 Tbsp (90 mL) pickling salt

Wash beans and cut off both ends. Pack lengthwise into hot sterilized 1-pint (475-mL) Mason jars, leaving ½ inch (1 cm) of headspace. Add 1 garlic clove, 1 dried cayenne pepper (or ¼ tsp/1 mL cayenne powder), 1 head dill (or 1 tsp/5 mL dill seeds) and 1 tsp (5 mL) peppercorns to each pint jar.

In a stainless-steel saucepan, mix the vinegar, water and salt, and bring to the boil, stirring to dissolve the salt. Ladle the brine over the beans in the jars, leaving ¼ inch (5 mm) of headspace. Follow the steps in How to Process High-Acid Foods (see page 78) and process in a boiling-water canner for 10 minutes. Let stand for 2 weeks before eating.

Makes six 1-pint (475-mL) jars

Pickled Crabapples

This recipe is a great solution for a tree loaded with crabapples in fall. Make sure to choose only the healthiest crabapples of uniform size.

4 cups (1 L) apple cider vinegar

2 cups (475 mL) light honey

1 Tbsp (15 mL) cinnamon

1 Tbsp (15 mL) cloves

1 Tbsp (15 mL) mace

1 Tbsp (15 mL) allspice

7 lb (3 kg) crabapples, washed and stemmed

Make a syrup of the vinegar, honey and spices, heating just enough to dissolve the honey. Leave to cool. Add the crabapples to the syrup and simmer gently, so that the fruit does not burst. Remove from heat and allow the apples to remain in the syrup overnight.

Next morning, pack the apples into sterilized jars and fill with the syrup to within ½ inch (1 cm) from the top. Process for 20 minutes in a boiling-water canner. See How to Process High-Acid Foods (see page 78).

Makes five 1-pint (475-mL) jars

Vegetable Antipasto VG GF

A delectable way to store your abundant garden harvest for festive occasions, antipasto is a savoury appetizer that pleases the palate before meals.

Note: Don't alter the ingredients or measurements of this recipe, because it has been formulated to be safely processed in a boiling-water canner.

2 cups (475 mL) raw cane sugar, lightly packed
3 Tbsp (45 mL) pickling salt
2 cups (475 mL) red wine vinegar
2 cups (475 mL) Tomato Paste (see page 73)
¼ cup (60 mL) Worcestershire sauce
2 Tbsp (30 mL) hot pepper sauce
5 garlic cloves, minced
1½ cups (350 mL) carrots, diced
2½ cups (600 mL) green beans, in ½ -inch (1-cm) pieces
2½ cups (600 mL) cauliflower, broken into small florets
2 cups (475 mL) onion, diced
2 cups (475 mL) red peppers, diced
2 cups (475 mL) green peppers, diced
1½ cups (350 mL) celery, chopped coarsely
2 cups (475 mL) zucchini, diced
3 Tbsp (45 mL) dried basil
1 Tbsp (15 mL) dried mustard powder

In a large saucepan, combine sugar, salt, vinegar, tomato paste, Worcestershire sauce, hot pepper sauce and garlic. Bring to the boil, stirring frequently. Stir in the carrots and cook for 2 minutes.

Add the remaining vegetables, basil and mustard, and bring to the boil. Cook gently over medium-high heat, stirring constantly. Ladle the antipasto into sterilized 1-pint (475-mL) Mason jars to within ½ inch (1 cm) from the top.

Process for 25 minutes. See How to Process High-Acid Foods (page 78). Store in a cool, dark place.

Makes seven 1-pint (475-mL) jars

Marinated Roasted Peppers VG GF

Roasting peppers makes them sweeter, more complex and wonderful in a host of recipes. Here's a good way to preserve a pepper harvest for use anytime.

4 lb (2 kg) sweet peppers

½ cup (125 mL) fresh lemon juice

1 cup (250 mL) white vinegar (5 percent)

½ cup (125 mL) extra virgin olive oil (plus additional for roasting peppers)

2 garlic cloves, quartered

1 tsp (5 mL) salt

Preheat the oven grill. Slice the peppers in half lengthwise and scoop out the seeds. Place the peppers, insides downward, on a baking pan. Position the oven rack so that the peppers in the pan are 5 inches (13 cm) away from the heat element. The surface of the peppers will blister and start to blacken. TIP: Rubbing the skin with olive oil helps the peppers to blister faster. Once the peppers have cooled enough to handle, gently peel off the blackened skin.

Bring the lemon juice, vinegar, olive oil, garlic and salt to the boil. Distribute the roasted peppers and garlic evenly among sterilized half-pint (250 mL) glass jars. Ladle the hot brine over the peppers, leaving ½ inch (1 cm) of headspace. Follow steps 1 to 11 in How to Process High-Acid Foods (see page 78). Leave the jars to cool at room temperature. When you hear them "pop" they will be sealed. Check seals before storing in a cool, dark place. Once opened, keep refrigerated.

Makes three ½-pint (250-mL) jars

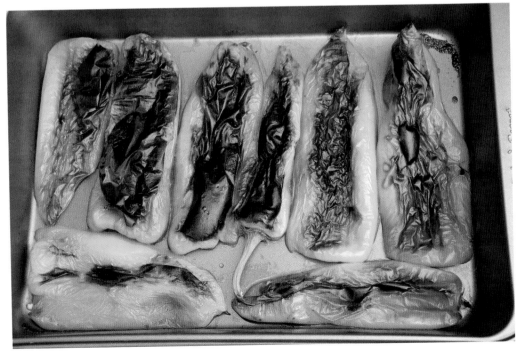

Roasted yellow peppers.

Pepper and Apple Chutney VG GF

Here's a fruity chutney that puts the flavour of summer back on your plate at any time of year.

- **2 large apples, peeled and chopped**
- **3 medium red peppers, diced**
- **2 medium onions, peeled and chopped**
- **2 garlic cloves, minced**
- **½ cup (125 mL) currants, or mix with raisins**
- **1 cup (250 mL) apple cider vinegar**
- **½ cup (125 mL) raspberry vinegar (see page 45)**
- **½ cup (125 mL) dry white wine**
- **2 cups (475 mL) water**
- **2 tsp (10 mL) black peppercorns**
- **1 tsp (5 mL) whole cloves**
- **1 cup (250 mL) brown sugar, firmly packed**

Combine apples, peppers, onions, garlic, currants, vinegars, wine and water in a large saucepan. Tie the peppercorns and cloves in a cheesecloth bag tied up with cotton string, and add to the pan. Bring to the boil, then simmer uncovered, stirring occasionally, for 15 minutes or until the apples and peppers are soft. Add the sugar and stir until it has dissolved. Bring to the boil and then simmer, stirring occasionally, for about 1½ hours or until thickened. Discard the cheesecloth bag. Pour the hot chutney into hot sterilized Mason jars, leaving ½ inch (1 cm) of headspace.

Follow steps 1 to 11 in How to Process High-Acid Foods (see page 78). Leave to cool. When you hear the jars "pop," the lids have sealed. Check the seals before storing.

Makes three 1-pint (475-mL) jars

Green Tomato Relish VG GF

This relish is a good way to use up all those end-of-the-season green tomatoes.

2.2 lb (1 kg) green tomatoes (about 12)

1 medium onion

2.2 lb (1 kg) pickling cucumbers

1 green pepper, seeded

¼ cup (60 mL) coarse salt

2 cups (475 mL) apple cider vinegar

1 cup (250 mL) white vinegar

1 tsp (5 mL) mustard seeds

½ tsp (2.5 mL) ground allspice

¼ tsp (1 mL) ground cinnamon

¼ tsp (1 mL) fresh-ground black pepper

1 cup (250 mL) brown sugar, packed tight

Combine the vegetables in a food processor and process until chopped into small pieces but not mushy. Sprinkle with salt and leave to stand for several hours. Rinse under cold water to remove salt and drain well.

Combine with vinegars and spices in a large saucepan. Bring to the boil and then simmer uncovered for 45 minutes. Add the sugar and stir over heat without boiling until the sugar has dissolved. Bring to the boil and boil uncovered for 15 minutes.

Follow steps 1 to 11 in How to Process High-Acid Foods (see page 78). Leave to cool. When you hear the jars "pop," the lids have sealed. Check the seals before storing.

Makes five 1-pint (475-mL) jars

Below: Cherry tomatoes.

Rhubarb Ginger Chutney VG GF

Here's a delicious chutney recipe for that prolific rhubarb harvest in early spring.

4 cups (1 L) 1-inch (2.5-cm) pieces of rhubarb

3 cups (700 mL) raw cane sugar, packed

2½ cups (600 mL) apple cider vinegar

2 onions, chopped

1 cup (250 mL) crystallized ginger, finely chopped

½ cup (125 mL) raisins

1 tsp (5 mL) cayenne pepper flakes

1 Tbsp (15 mL) mustard seed

1 tsp (5 mL) pickling spices

½ tsp (2.5 mL) sea salt

In a heavy saucepan, combine all the ingredients. Over medium heat bring to the boil, stirring. Turn down the heat and leave to simmer for 1½ hours, stirring from time to time until thickened. Pack the hot chutney into hot sterilized 1-pint (475-mL) Mason jars through the funnel, leaving ½ inch (1 cm) of headspace.

Follow steps 1 to 11 in How to Process High-Acid Foods (see page 78). Leave the lids to seal as they cool. Wait for the pop! Check seals before storing in a cool, dark place for up to 12 months.

Makes two 1-pint (475-mL) jars

Zucchini Salsa VG GF

Here's a refreshing way to use up excess summer zucchini that just keep coming!

10 cups (2.5 L) zucchini, grated

4 medium onions, chopped

2 green peppers, seeded and diced

2 red peppers, seeded and diced

4 jalapeno peppers, seeded and diced

¼ cup (60 mL) pickling salt or sea salt

Mix the above ingredients together and leave them to sit overnight.

Drain off the excess liquid.

2 Tbsp (30 mL) dry mustard powder

4 garlic cloves, minced

1 Tbsp (15 mL) cumin powder

1 Tbsp (15 mL) turmeric

1 tsp (5 mL) hot pepper flakes

2 cups (475 mL) red wine or apple cider vinegar

1 cup (250 mL) brown sugar

1 bunch fresh cilantro, chopped

6 cups (1.4 L) chopped tomatoes (or use two 28-oz/796-gr cans of tomatoes)

1 cup (250 mL) Garden Tomato Sauce (see page 205)

½ cup (125 mL) Tomato Paste (see page 73)

In a large saucepan, mix together the above ingredients and stir in the vegetables. Bring to the boil for 5 minutes, stirring constantly. Hot pack the salsa into sterilized 1-pint (475-mL) jars, leaving ½ inch (1 cm) of headspace.

Process at a rolling boil in a water canner for 30 minutes. See How to Process High-Acid Foods (page 78).

Makes eleven 1-pint (475-mL) jars

Rules of Thumb for Jam and Jelly Making

- Sterilize all jars, rings and lids in boiling water before filling.
- If a jar does not process correctly and has a lid that has not sealed or does not pop down in the centre after cooling, it should be refrigerated and used immediately to avoid potential poisoning from *C. botulinum* bacteria (botulism).
- Avoid using more than 4.4 lb (2 kg) fruit at once for any jam recipe. Larger quantities will affect the setting process.

Q What's the difference between jellies, jams and preserves and conserves?

A Jellies are created using the juice of a fruit, or by making a tea from flowers or leaves of a plant (like clover and mint jelly).

The terms "jam" and "preserve" are often used interchangeably as both use macerated fruit. Preserves tend to have a chunkier texture and conserves contain whole fruit but all are cooked with sweeteners and often pectin, and then preserved in sealed jars, or in a boiling-water canner for longer storage.

Roasted Red Pepper and Chili Jelly VG GF

This jelly is sweet and tangy with a bite from the chili peppers. It's one of our favourites with egg and rice dishes, and goes perfectly with a plate of cheese and crackers.

8 red peppers, roasted (see page 82)

1 onion, roughly chopped

4 red chili peppers, halved and seeded

2 garlic cloves, chopped

1 cup (250 mL) water

1 cup (250 mL) white wine vinegar

1½ tsp (7 mL) sea salt

2¼ cups (535 mL) sugar

2 tsp calcium water (prepared from the calcium included in the box of pectin)

1½ tsp (7 mL) Pomona's Universal Pectin (see page 89)

Purée the roasted peppers, onion, garlic, chilies and water in a food processor until coarsely chopped. Press the purée through a sieve using a wooden spoon, extracting as much as you can (ideally 3 cups/700 mL). In a saucepan, mix purée, vinegar, salt and calcium water. Mix ½ cup (125 mL) sugar with pectin and stir into the liquid until well dissolved. Add remaining sugar and bring to the boil, stirring vigorously for 4 minutes.

Distribute the jelly evenly among the 1-pint (475-mL) Mason jars, leaving ½ inch (1 cm) of headspace. Follow steps 1 to 11 in How to Process High-Acid Foods (see page 78). Leave to cool. When you hear the jars "pop," the lids have sealed. Check the seals before storing in a cool, dark place.

Makes three 1-pint (475-mL) jars

1-2-3 Quick and Easy Jam VG GF

This is the fastest, easiest jam to make using berries with seeds on the outside, e.g., strawberries, raspberries and blackberries. The secret is to beat the jam like heck in all three stages of production to release the pectin in the seeds. TIP: Fresh-picked berries are best, not overripe, and it's best to make small batches (up to 6 cups/1.4 L) at a time.

1 cup (250 mL) berries

1 cup (250 mL) granulated sugar

Boil the berries without sugar for 1 minute, while whisking.

Remove from the heat, add the sugar and bring back to the boil, whisking for 2 minutes.

Remove from the heat and whisk for another 3 minutes.

Optional: Remove the pits and seeds by putting the jam through a food mill (see page 32).

Pour the hot jam into hot sterilized 1-pint (475-mL) Mason jars. Follow steps 1 to 11 in How to

Process High-Acid Foods (see page 78). Turn the jars upside down for 10 minutes. Leave to cool. When the jam thickens and the jars "pop," the lids have sealed. This jam will store for up to 12 months in a cool, dark place. Refrigerate once opened.

Makes two 1-pint (475-mL) jars

Below: 1-2-3 Quick and Easy Jam. Turn berries into yummy jam in no time!

Pomona's Cherry Jam VG GF

I use Pomona's Universal Pectin to set jams and jellies. Ordinary fruit pectins require that the jam or jelly be 55 to 85 percent sugar to set firmly. Pomona's Universal is a low-methoxyl pectin (100-percent pure-citrus pectin extracted from citrus peel—it's also gluten-free and vegan). You can cut back or eliminate sugar because the jelling power is activated using calcium (included in the box), not sugar.

8 cups (2 L) sweet cherries, pitted and macerated

2 large juicy lemons, juiced

1 cup (250 mL) water

2½ Tbsp (38 mL) calcium water (prepared from the calcium included in the box of pectin)

1 cup (250 mL) honey

2½ Tbsp (40 mL) Pomona's Universal Pectin

Put the macerated cherries, lemon juice, calcium water and water in a large saucepan, and bring to the boil. Simmer for about 5 minutes, until the cherry juices start to flow freely. Mix the honey with the pectin powder and add it to the saucepan. Bring to the boil and boil for 1 minute, stirring vigorously until pectin is fully dissolved. Remove from heat.

Pour the jam into hot sterilized 1-pint (475-mL) Mason jars. Follow steps 1 to 11 in How to Process High-Acid Foods (see page 78). Turn the jars upside down for 10 minutes, then turn lid side up and leave them to cool. When the jam thickens and the jars "pop," the lids have sealed. This jam will store for up to 12 months in a cool, dark place. Refrigerate once opened.

Makes five 1-pint (475-mL) jars

'Stella' sweet cherries.

Cherry Conserves VG GF

You won't need much of this gooey delight to elicit sighs of pleasure from around the table! I use it as a fruity topping on desserts or scones, or as a sweet filling in sponge sandwich cakes.

- **1 lb (454 gr) sour cherries**
- **1 lb (454 gr) sugar**

or

- **1 lb (454 gr) sweet cherries**
- **¾ lb (340 gr) sugar**

Wash, pit and stem the cherries. TIP: If you own a cherry tree, buy a cherry pitter, which will make this job fun. In a stainless-steel saucepan, place the pitted cherries in single layers, covering each layer with sugar and ending with a layer of sugar on top. Cover the saucepan with a lid and leave the cherries to stand for 8 to 10 hours or overnight.

Slowly bring this mixture to the boil, stirring frequently. Then reduce the heat and simmer on low for 20 minutes, stirring occasionally until it thickens. If the conserves have not set after 25 to 30 minutes, do a gel test to see if the conserves need more time to cook.

Gel Test

Place a teaspoonful of the hot mixture on a cold plate, and put it in the freezer to cool quickly. After cooling, push the mixture up with your forefinger. If it wrinkles and keeps its shape, you'll know the jam, jelly or conserve will set once it cools.

Pour the hot cherry conserves into hot sterilized 1-pint (475-mL) Mason jars. Follow Steps 1 to 11 in How to Process High-Acid Foods (see page 78). The conserves will thicken as they cool, and the lids will seal with a "pop"!

Makes two 1-pint (475-mL) jars

Golden's Rosehip Syrup   VG GF

Rosehips are the vitamin C–rich fruits of roses. It's best to harvest rosehips after a few hard frosts, as then they are easier to pick and process. The perfumed aroma of rosehips with apple makes a truly delicate syrup.

2 cups (475 mL) rosehips, tops and ends cut off
1 cup (250 mL) fresh apple juice
Zest of ½ lemon

Put the rosehips in a saucepan with a little water to prevent sticking. TIP: Use as little water as possible to get the best flavour. Bring to the boil, reduce heat and simmer gently until soft, without stirring, for 45 to 60 minutes. Watch out, they burn easily! Let cool slightly and sieve out ALL the seeds. TIP: Using a food mill (see page 32) is the easiest way to do this.

Put the sieved rosehips into a clean saucepan,

and add the fresh apple juice. Cook gently for 10 to 15 minutes, and add the zest.

Either store the syrup in the refrigerator, or hot pack it into sterilized ½-pint (250-mL) Mason jars. Follow How to Process High-Acid Foods (see page 78) for longer storage.

Makes two ½-pint (250-mL) jars

FERMENTATION

Our ancestors used lactic-acid fermentation to preserve food for times when fresh supplies were not available. In traditional cultures, many foods were preserved this way: fish as pastes; grains as sourdough bread, beer, miso and soy sauce; beans as tempeh; dairy products as yogourt, cheese and kefir; beverages as beer and kombucha; vegetables as sauerkraut and kim chi; and fruit as wine.

During the process of fermentation, the starches and sugars in the food are converted by beneficial bacteria to lactic acid, a natural preservative that inhibits putrefying bacteria. Our ancestors used to rely on this technique for preserving food, but now freezing, canning and refrigeration have mostly replaced it. As a result, people are no longer ingesting a steady supply of beneficial bacteria, which prevent the proliferation of viruses and "bad" bacteria, and keep intestinal tracts healthy and immune systems strong.

Modern researchers are just beginning to understand the incalculable health benefits that fermented foods convey to human immunity, intestinal health and general well-being. Intestinal flora are thought to influence a wide array of human health issues, and there is speculation that many modern diseases are in part caused by abandoning this ancient practice of fermentation.

Health Benefits of Lacto-Fermented Foods

- They normalize the acidity of the stomach. If the acidity is insufficient, they stimulate the acid-producing glands of the stomach. In cases where the acidity is too high, they have the opposite effect. This means that lacto-fermented foods would be wise to include in your diet if you have ulcers, irritable bowel syndrome, lack of appetite, gas or indigestion.
- Lactic acid activates the secretions of the pancreas, which are important in preventing diabetes.
- People who have taken, or are taking, antibiotics benefit tremendously from regular consumption of fermented foods, because they help to restore the balance of healthy bacteria in the digestive tract.
- Lacto-fermented foods are high in vitamin C. They can be cooked, but they are best enjoyed raw to retain their many vitamins and enzymes.
- Lactic-acid fermentation decreases the level of phytic acid naturally present in grains. Phytic acid is an anti-nutrient that binds up minerals and prevents their full absorption in the gut.

What are Probiotics and Prebiotics?

PROBIOTICS

Probiotics are foods containing live micro-organisms that recolonize the human digestive tract with beneficial bacteria that synthesize vitamins, absorb nutrients and keep pathogens at bay. They interact directly with the immune system for overall health.

Good Sources
- Yogourt
- Kombucha
- Water Kefir
- Fermented Vegetables

PREBIOTICS

Prebiotics work synergistically with probiotics by promoting the proliferation of beneficial bacteria in the digestive system. A diet rich in prebiotics feeds intestinal flora. Humans throughout history ate more of the foods rich in prebiotics than they do today.

Good Sources
- Asparagus
- Chicory
- Endive
- Fresh Dandelion Greens
- Frisée
- Garlic
- Onions
- Radicchio
- Sunchokes
- Wheat and Sprouted Wheat

Homemade Yogourt

Yogourt originated centuries ago from traditional Eastern European foods. Beneficial bacteria turn milk into yogourt by lactic-acid fermentation; the bacteria metabolize lactose, a sugar naturally present in milk. The result is a thicker product with a tangy, slightly mouth-puckering effect. Yogourt is lower in carbohydrates and higher in B vitamins, including folic acid, than regular whole milk. Furthermore, many people who are lactose-intolerant find they can eat yogourt without a reaction.

Most yogourt is made with cow's milk, but sheep and goat milk are also used. The flavour and consistency of the yogourt will vary according to the region where it's made, because the fat and protein content of the milk and the bacterial culture will differ. If sheep's or goat's milk is used, it results in a richer, creamier yogourt with a consistency similar to custard.

Raw Milk Yogourt GF

Raw milk is a sort of Holy Grail for traditional-foods enthusiasts. It preserves the enzymatic and probiotic components of the fresh milk in the resulting yogourt.

TIP: Because of the presence of beneficial bacteria in raw milk, the yogourt starter degrades over time, so it may be necessary to purchase fresh starter culture periodically to protect the quality of the resulting yogourt.

To prepare: Sterilize a 2-quart (2-L) Mason jar, fill it with hot water and leave it to stand. Half-fill a pot, large enough to accommodate the upright jar, with water and bring it to the boil. Remove from heat and leave the pot to stand with the lid on while you prepare the yogourt.

5 cups (1.2 L) raw goat, sheep or cow milk

1 cup (250 mL) yogourt culture at room temperature

(Purchase Bulgarian or Greek yogourt as culture, or use yogourt from a previous batch)

Heat the milk to 110F (43C), using a kitchen thermometer to check the temperature. Not overheating the milk will preserve the fat-soluble vitamins, enzymes and naturally occurring beneficial bacteria. Add the yogourt culture, whisking while blending together. Bring back to the temperature of 110F (43C). Pour into the hot 2-quart (2-L) Mason jar, leaving ½ inch (1 cm) of headspace, and seal the jar with a snap lid, secured with the metal ring.

Sit the jar inside the pot of hot water and cover the pot with the lid. Put the covered pot inside a cardboard box (or cooler), and insulate it with towels. Close the flaps on the box to seal the heat in.

Leave to stand for 8 to 12 hours or overnight, until the yogourt has thickened. Remove the warm jar of yogourt and chill in the refrigerator. The yogourt will keep refrigerated for up to 2 weeks.

Makes 8 cups (2 L)

Labneh GF

Labneh is yogourt cheese of Middle Eastern origin, where it is rolled into small balls and served with olive oil. Labneh is simple to make and is rich in beneficial bacteria.

4 cups (1 L) of fresh yogourt, preferably raw milk
½ tsp (2.5 mL) unrefined sea salt
Extra virgin olive oil, as needed
Fresh herbs such as basil, dill, sweet marjoram, parsley or oregano

Fold a piece of cheesecloth in quarters, set it inside a fine-mesh sieve and set the sieve above a bowl. Mix the yogourt with the salt, and pour into the cheesecloth-lined sieve. After the initial straining (10 minutes), fold the cheesecloth into the centre, and twist it into a tight bundle, keeping it tight as you tie it up with an elastic band. TIP: Don't throw the whey away. This liquid is rich in beneficial bacteria. Use it to soak grains to render them more digestible, as a starter for other fermented foods or as an addition to smoothies for extra probiotics in your diet. Whey keeps refrigerated for up to 6 months.

Hang the cheesecloth from a hook, with a bowl beneath to catch dripping whey. Hanging from a hook speeds up straining. Hang at room temperature for at least 12 hours, preferably 18 to 24 hours for best results. Remove the cheesecloth and find labneh, which is like cream cheese. Roll the labneh into small walnut-sized balls of cheese, and put the balls into a Mason jar. Cover with the olive oil and add your choice of fresh herbs for flavouring. Store in the refrigerator.

Makes ¾ cup (175 mL)

Pickled Pepperoncini Peppers

The process of lactic-acid fermentation is relatively straightforward, but there are a few things to be aware of to ensure success. This recipe for pickled pepperoncini peppers using the fermentation method tells you what you need to know.

4 packed cups (1 L) pepperoncini peppers

Brine

2 cups (475 mL) water

2 Tbsp (30 mL) regular, white wine or apple cider vinegar

1 Tbsp (15 mL) pickling salt

Optional: 2 tsp (10 mL) unpasteurized lactic culture (from sauerkraut or a previous batch of peppers) or whey from the top of plain yogourt

Bring the brine to the boil, stir until the salt dissolves and leave to cool.

Wash the pepperoncini peppers, leaving the stems on and the seeds in, and slice down each pepper lengthwise to let the air out and the brine in. Pack the peppers into a wide-mouthed 1-quart (1-L) sterilized Mason jar, filling the jar as much as possible—the more peppers the better. Too few peppers will hinder the fermentation process, so switch to a smaller jar if you don't have enough for a tight pack.

Cover the peppers to the very top of the jar with the brine solution, saving some brine for later. You can save extra brine in the fridge for up to a week.

Before sealing the jar, get all the air out of the pepper cavities by tapping the jar against the counter every few hours to dislodge air bubbles. Then refill the jar with the remaining brine. Repeat this process until the pepper cavities are full of brine.

Seal the jar with a lid and a metal ring, but don't put the ring on too tightly. If it's too loose, air may leak back in after fermentation ceases. If it's too tight, the lid may buckle or the jar may burst.

If fermentation fails to begin, give it a kick-start

by adding 2 teaspoons of unpasteurized lactic culture or whey.

Set the jar in a warm place, about 70–90F (21–32C) as lactic acid bacteria prefer heat. Fermentation can take place in cooler conditions, but it will be slower. Put a plate under the jar—just in case things bubble over and wait at least 2 weeks before consuming.

Store finished peppers in the refrigerator and eat within one month of opening.

Makes one 1-quart (1-L) jar

Horseradish Sauce

Fermenting horseradish makes a healthy probiotic condiment that is imbued with beneficial bacteria and also leaves your taste buds tingling!

I was leery of making horseradish sauce when I first read the dire warnings about chopping this odourless root. When horseradish releases its active ingredient isothiocyanate into the air, it burns the eyes and irritates the sinuses. So I opted for a calm, sunny day to dig out two large horseradish roots and set up an outdoor table for this auspicious event. To my relief, I suffered none of the above-mentioned effects, and found this pungent sauce a breeze to make. However, best beware!

1 cup (250 mL) horseradish root (2 large roots), peeled and chopped
1½ tsp (7 mL) sea salt, unrefined
½ cup (125 mL) fresh whey, or 1 packet purchased starter culture for fresh vegetables
A few tablespoons filtered water, as necessary

Remove the woody interior fibres from the root and chop into sections small enough to feed through the funnel of a food processor. Add the sea salt and ¼ cup (60 mL) of whey (or all the packet starter culture). Process for 1 minute to combine everything. I used ½ cup (125 mL) of the brine from our fermented peppers as whey. You could also use 2 tsp (10 mL) unpasteurized lactic culture from sauerkraut or kim chi.

Add the remaining ¼ cup (60 mL) whey (and filtered water if needed), and continue to process for another 3 to 4 minutes, until a smooth paste forms. TIP: This is when you minimize in-breaths!

Put a funnel over a ½-pint (250-mL) Mason jar, and use a spatula to spoon the horseradish sauce into the jar, tapping to level it, and adding whey or water so that the sauce is covered.

Cover the jar with a snap lid and secure it loosely with a metal ring. Leave to ferment in a warm place for at least 3 and up to 7 days. Keep stored in the refrigerator, where it will stay good for several months.

Makes 1 cup (250 mL)

Below: Freshly dug horseradish roots.

Creamy Horseradish Dip `VG*` `GF`

This vegetable dip with a bite is perfect to serve with crudités, chips or crackers!

3 Tbsp (45 mL) horseradish sauce
¼ cup (60 mL) sour cream
1 tsp (5 mL) prepared Dijon mustard
Splash of Worcestershire sauce
Pinch of salt to taste

Blend together into a smooth dip.

Makes ½ cup (125 mL)

* if you use soy sour cream

Sauerkraut

Sauerkraut is a centuries-old health food that provides a good source of probiotics in the diet. The salt pulls water out of the cabbage and creates the brine in which the cabbage ferments and sours without rotting. The salt also keeps the cabbage crunchy, by preventing the organisms and enzymes that soften it. A rough guideline to follow is 3 Tbsp (45 mL) of salt to 5 lb (2.3 kg) of cabbage.

Mason jars work fine for small quantities of fermented food but are not optimally suited to larger batches. Because fermentation is an anaerobic process, the key to success is that the food rests below liquid. When fermented foods are exposed to air, they risk being contaminated by microbes, yeasts and moulds. If fermented vegetables go mouldy, it is probably because they were not fully submerged in the brine. Slow cookers are ideal for fermenting foods, because they have lids that allow the gases that build up to escape, while preventing oxygen from getting in to cause spoilage.

Henry harvests 'January King' cabbages, a bumper crop that matured in June!

Easy Sauerkraut `VG` `GF`

Finely shredded cabbage and salt is all you need for fermentation, which results in a slightly sour, crunchy cabbage salad, good eaten cold or hot and just so good for digestive flora! TIP: Use the juice (left over after the sauerkraut is eaten), because it is an unparalleled digestive tonic. Making fermented food is the perfect thing to do with all those cabbages that head up in the spring and fall season.

1 medium-sized head (2.2 lb/1 kg) green cabbage

4 tsp (20 mL) unrefined sea salt

Remove the outer leaves and shred the cabbage into thin slices. Because I prefer sauerkraut that is sliced on the finer rather than coarser side, I use my mandoline (see page 29). Put the cabbage into a large bowl, sprinkling it with salt and pounding it for about 10 minutes, using a clean wine bottle or pestle, until it releases its juices. This juice becomes the brine that the sauerkraut ferments in.

Pack cabbage lightly into a clean, sterilized 1-quart (1-L) Mason jar, until the juice covers the cabbage. Place the snap lid on and loosely secure with the metal ring. Set the jar in a bowl to catch the bubbling liquid as the cabbage ferments. After 7 to 10 days, the cabbage

should stop fermenting, which indicates that the sauerkraut is done. The sealed jar stores refrigerated for up to 6 months.

For Longer Storage

Press fermented sauerkraut down with a wooden spoon to remove any gas bubbles. Make a brine of 4 tsp (20 mL) sea salt to 4 cups (1 L) water, and fill the jar leaving ½ inch (1 cm) of headspace. TIP: Use filtered water, as chlorine hampers fermentation.

Process in a water canner for 30 minutes. See Home Canning (page 77).

Makes one 1-quart (1-L) jar

Slow Cooker Sauerkraut VG GF

Here's a more traditional method of making sauerkraut.

2 medium heads green cabbage (5 lb/2.3 kg), washed, cored and finely shredded
2 Tbsp (30 mL) unrefined sea salt

One of the following:
2 Tbsp (30 mL) juniper berries
2 Tbsp (30 mL) fresh dill, chopped
1 Tbsp (15 mL) caraway seeds
1 Tbsp (15 mL) fresh ginger root, minced
10 black peppercorns

Toss the shredded cabbage and salt together in a large mixing bowl and pound for about 10 minutes, using a clean wine bottle or pestle, until the cabbage becomes limp and releases its juices.

Transfer cabbage to a ceramic or stoneware crockpot and pack in as tightly as possible, eliminating any air bubbles, until the cabbage is completely covered by the liquid. Place a clean, heavy plate on top of the cabbage to keep it submerged under liquid as it ferments.

Put the lid on the slow cooker, and leave it undisturbed at room temperature for 7 to 10 days.

Test to see if the sauerkraut is done to your liking. If not, leave for another few days and test again, up to a maximum of 3 weeks. Add herb or spice of your choice and transfer the fermented sauerkraut into sterilized, airtight glass jars and store in the refrigerator, where it should keep for 6 months. TIP: If scum appears in the brine, simply spoon off all you can and don't worry about it.

Makes 8 cups (2 L)

Nourishing Traditions Kim Chi.

Kim Chi

Do as Koreans do, and eat some healthy kim chi every day. Kim chi has a refreshing, crunchy, tangy texture and is so much revered in Korea that when you take a photo there they say, "Kim chi!" Kim chi is a traditional Korean condiment made of fermented vegetables. You can try different combinations of ingredients by adding turnips, radishes, red cabbage or other vegetables readily found in the winter garden. It is quick and easy to prepare, and the only equipment you need is a large stainless-steel bowl and glass Mason jars. Adding salt prevents the vegetables from rotting in the first few days of the process, until enough lactic acid is produced to preserve the kim chi.

Kim chi is lacto-fermented by beneficial bacteria, lactobacilli, which are naturally present on vegetables and produce lactic acid that pickles and preserves the vegetables. This makes kim chi a "live" probiotic food that introduces healthful bacteria into the digestive system, and also provides valuable vitamins and minerals.

Nourishing Traditions Kim Chi

Thanks to Sally Fallon and Mary G. Enig for permission to share this recipe. It is not only delicious but exemplifies what they advocate—eating to nourish the body rather than to just satisfy the senses.

1 medium head green cabbage, cored and shredded

1 large onion, chopped

1 cup (250 mL) carrots, shredded or cut into thin coins

1 Tbsp (15 mL) fresh ginger root, grated

3 cloves garlic, minced

½ tsp (2.5 mL) dried red pepper flakes (or more for extra hotness!)

1 Tbsp (15 mL) sea salt

4 Tbsp (60 mL) whey* (if not available, use an additional 1 Tbsp/15 mL salt)

Place all the ingredients in a large bowl (a ceramic crock works well). Pound them for about 10 minutes with a wooden pestle or empty wine bottle to release the juices. Put the kim chi into a 2-quart (2-L) Mason jar (or a ceramic crock), stuffing the jar as tightly as possible, until juice comes over the top of the cabbage. Leave 1 inch (2.5 cm) of headspace in the jar.

Put the snap lid on loosely, lightly securing with the metal ring, and place the jar in a bowl allowing for gases or liquid to escape. Leave to ferment for 7 to 10 days at 50F (10C). When fermentation stops, the kim chi is done. It will keep stored in the refrigerator for up to 6 months.

Makes 8 cups (2 L)

* Two options to get whey are to make Labneh (Yogourt Cheese) (see page 94) or Pickled Pepperoncini Peppers (see page 95).

Kombucha Tea—Elixir of Life

Kombucha tea is thought to date back to the Chinese Qin Dynasty of 221 BC when Zen masters regarded it as the "elixir of life"—a source of revitalizing energy that harmonized body, mind and spirit to create balance and vitality.

Kombucha (pronounced kom-BOO-cha) is a fermented tea, either green or black depending on your preference. During fermentation, essential nutrients, enzymes, probiotics, amino acids, antioxidants and polyphenols form. Depending on brewing method, Kombucha can be mildly alcoholic.

Kombucha has an agreeably sparkling, slightly sour and refreshing taste. For a health tonic, aim to drink three glasses a day—on an empty stomach in the morning, after a meal in the course of the day and a short time before going to bed, gradually building up to the goal of ⅔ cup (160 mL) three times a day.

Kombucha has a home-brewing safety track record of two thousand years. The contamination of the culture (or scoby) by mould is not a problem if normal standards of kitchen hygiene are observed.

On the left is a commercially bottled Kombucha beverage. The jar on the right contains a scoby—the Kombucha culture.

Kombucha is acidic (with a pH of 3) so it has its own protection against pathogens. If mould does occur, dispose of the culture and brew, just as you would other mouldy food.

How to Brew Kombucha Tea VG GF

We normally make a 1-gallon (4-L) glass jar of tea at a time, but you can also make a 1-quart (1-L) jar of Kombucha tea. The gallon takes up to 2 weeks to brew, but the smaller jar will be ready in only 1 week. Metal containers, other than stainless steel, should never be used because the acids formed may react with metal.

- **12 cups (3 L) pure well or filtered water**
- **5 teabags or 5 tsp (25 mL) leaves of green tea or black tea**
- **1 cup (250 mL) granulated white sugar**
- **½ cup (125 mL) Kombucha reserve liquid (get some from a friend or from a store-bought bottle of unpasteurized, unflavored Kombucha—select a bottle with visible masses of solid material)**

In a large stainless-steel saucepan, combine the water, tea and sugar. Bring to the boil, stirring occasionally using a wooden spoon, until the sugar has dissolved. Remove the saucepan from the heat, cover and leave to steep for 10 to 15 minutes.

Remove teabags, or sieve tea leaves, and leave to cool, covered, to a lukewarm temperature no higher than 77F (25C), so the scoby is not destroyed in too hot a solution. Pour the liquid into a sterilized 1-gallon (4-L) glass jar. When preparing your first batch of Kombucha, add the liquid that comes with the mother scoby. On later batches, add ½ cup (125 mL) reserved Kombucha liquid.

With clean and rinsed hands (hygiene is critical), place the scoby in the jar, where it may sink to the bottom. Sometimes the culture floats, sometimes it sinks; both are okay. When the scoby sinks, a new culture (baby) will grow on the surface of the tea.

Cover the jar with some cheesecloth, or other breathable cloth that allows air in and keeps dust and flies out. Secure the cloth in place using a rubber band around the neck of the jar. Kombucha needs a warm place, the temperature should not fall below 68F (20C), and on no account should it be moved. The culture works in darkness, and may be damaged by exposure to bright sunlight, so a shady place for fermentation is best.

It takes between 12 and 18 days until fermentation is complete. Good Kombucha has a pH of 3, which has a healthy alkalizing effect on the body. You can use pH strips to test the acidity of the final product, or you can trust your taste buds to check that it is vinegary enough. If a sweeter, sparkling drink is preferred, drink the Kombucha just after fermentation slows down— the longer you leave it fermenting, the more acidic and sour it will become.

When Kombucha has attained the right degree of acidity, remove the mother and baby scoby

with clean hands. Clean the scoby under running water, and as long as there is no mould, it can be refrigerated in some reserve liquid in a sterilized glass jar. A scoby will continue to propagate until it gradually turns dark brown, when it should be discarded and replaced with a new one.

The Kombucha can now be poured through a stainless-steel funnel into glass bottles, which should be filled to the brim and stoppered securely. Keep ½ cup (125 mL) Kombucha as a reserve starter to make the next batch. A certain amount of sediment is normal due to growth of yeasts, and the sediment can accompany the scoby to assist fermentation.

For the best taste, allow this drink to mature for at least 5 days after being bottled. The airtight bottles trap gas produced by the yeast that continues to feed on fruit sugar, thus a sparkling effervescent drink results. TIP: It's a good idea to open bottles cautiously to let the fizz out slowly.

Kombucha keeps well for months. There's no need to worry about explosions because the yeast stops gas production at a certain point. However, it is advisable to keep the beverage in a cool place.

Makes five 1-quart (1-L) glass bottles*

* glass bottles need stoppers

How to Flavour Kombucha Tea

Whether you flavour your tea is up to you, but there are lots of ways to change the resulting taste and experience. When bottling Kombucha, add the flavour to the bottle and then add the tea. Use airtight, resealable glass bottles.

Choose from the following:
- Fresh fruit such as sliced pears, fresh peaches or blueberries
- Fruit juices
- Herbs such as rosemary, thyme or lavender
- Macerated cranberries or dried cherries
- Slices of crystallized ginger
- Spirulina or chlorella

If adding fruit juice, add in a ratio of 20 percent juice: 80 percent Kombucha tea.

(Increasing the amount of juice makes the Kombucha sweeter.)

Kefir Fruit Juice VG GF

Kefir is made with "grains" that consist of colonies of yeast and bacteria strained out at the end of fermentation and used for future batches. Lactobacilli bacteria and yeast combine to give kefir effervescence, as well as a 1-percent alcohol content!

These grains were once treasured by people who kept them, and were selectively handed down through generations. Now you can buy kefir grains in health food stores to get started growing your own.

¼ cup (60 mL) of kefir grains for every quart (1 L) of juice

2–4 Tbsp (30–60 mL) raw cane sugar

6 berries, slightly crushed to release juices (or orange, lemon and ginger slices)

Filtered water or pure well water

Optional: Use coconut water and just add kefir grains—no sugar required! Make ginger lime juice by adding 1 lime quartered and squeezed with 4 Tbsp (60 mL) of grated ginger root in a tea ball.

Put the kefir grains into a cheesecloth bag. Tie up the top with cotton string and rinse in a bowl of filtered water. (Grains require fluoride- and chloride-free water.)

Using a wooden spoon (acidic reaction happens with metal), pour water into a ceramic bowl and stir in the sugar so that it is well dissolved. Fill a 1-quart (1-L) sterilized glass Mason jar to ½ inch (1 cm) from the top with this water. Place the bag of grains into the jar and the fruit, leaving ½ inch (1 cm) of headspace for the grains to ferment.

Put on the snap lid, and tighten loosely with the metal band to seal, but not so tight as to prevent gases from escaping during fermentation. Let the jar sit in a warm place at 70F (21C) and above for 48 hours. After 48 hours, bubbles should have formed on the top of the liquid, and the water will be lighter in colour. Loosen the lid carefully (do not shake the jar), test through a straw to see if it is to your liking or leave to ferment a bit longer.

When ready, remove the fruit from the liquid

(fermented fruit can be eaten), and compost any debris. Place a funnel into a well-rinsed bottle. (I use recycled kombucha bottles with caps.) Line the funnel with layers of cheesecloth and slowly pour the liquid into the bottle through the funnel to capture the kefir grains. Store capped bottles of fermented kefir water in the fridge. TIP: If you want kefir that is more fermented, leave the sealed bottles out for another 48 hours before refrigeration.

Store the grains in a glass jar with enough filtered water to cover, and 1 Tbsp (15 mL) raw cane sugar to feed them. They do not need to be rinsed before storage. Kefir grains can be stored in the fridge for a few weeks. Grains need to be rinsed in filtered water once a week, and should be creamy white in colour, unless they have been discoloured by berries. If mould develops, or there is any strange discoloration of the grains, discard them and do not use them again.

Makes 4 cups (1 L)

Sourdough Starters

Starters bring tangy flavour and crunch to breads that they leaven, as well as pancakes and baked goods. The easiest way to start is to buy a starter culture made from domesticated yeast rather than wild yeasts. Or you can make your own.

Keeping Starters

Storing the culture in the refrigerator lowers the requirement for feeding. Keeping the starter chilled slows down the growth of yeast and bacteria, but does not stop it completely, so it still needs to be fed once a week. A starter at room temperature 70F (21C) needs feeding every 6 to 8 hours! If the starter volume decreases, the yeast has run out of food and is dying off. Hurry—it's time for a feeding!

Feeding Tips

It's best not to starve the starter. Feed the starter at least 12 hours before you plan to use it. A feeding usually consists of adding amounts of flour and water equal to the the size of the starter. For example, if you have 1 cup (250 mL) of starter, stir in 1 cup (250 mL) flour and 1 cup (250 mL) of water. (You may need to adjust quantities slightly to maintain consistency.)

TIP: A good starter is worth sharing—if you dry it first you can easily send it to friends and family in the mail, or save it for yourself (it keeps 2 to 3 months dried). Drying is as simple as spreading the starter in a thin layer on a cookie sheet (lined with parchment paper), and allowing it to dry at room temperature for 3 days. To restart the culture, crumble the starter into warm water and begin regular feeding.

Make-Your-Own Starter

You can create your own "original" starter culture using the yeast and bacteria that are naturally around us in our environment.

2 cups (475 mL) all-purpose, whole wheat or whole rye flour
2 cups (475 mL) water, non-chlorinated (leave tap water out in open to air for 24 hours to evaporate chlorine)

Combine the flour and water in a bowl and stir until well blended. Cover loosely with cheesecloth and leave to sit until bubbly (2 to 3 days). If no bubbles appear after 3 to 5 days, discard and try again. Your starter should resemble a spongy, thick batter, with a tangy aroma. Starters sometimes separate into clear liquid and flour. If this happens, just stir together before use.

If the starter smells bad, turns mouldy or changes colour, throw it out. Store the starter in a covered glass or ceramic container, at room temperature, or refrigerate. When you accumulate more starter than you need, pour a few cups away before feeding it.

Makes 4 cups (1 L)

Berry Sourdough Pancakes

Now that you have your starter, you can enjoy these fluffy, fruity pancakes. You can use any berries in season for this recipe or make bumbleberry pancakes by combining different ones. Make sure to feed the sourdough the evening before you plan to make the pancakes so it is active and bubbly.

1½ cups (350 mL) all-purpose flour

3 Tbsp (45 mL) raw cane sugar

1½ tsp (7 mL) baking soda

½ tsp (2 mL) sea salt

1 cup (250 mL) milk

1 cup (250 mL) active, bubbly sourdough starter

2 large eggs

⅓ cup (80 mL) butter, melted

½ tsp (2 mL) pure vanilla extract

Vegetable oil for the griddle

Toppings

1¼ cups (300 mL) fresh blueberries, raspberries, strawberries, cherries, tayberries or loganberries

Butter

Maple syrup

In a bowl, sift together the dry ingredients—flour, sugar, baking soda and salt. In another bowl, whisk together the wet ingredients—eggs, milk, sourdough starter, melted butter and vanilla—until well blended. Add the wet to the dry ingredients, stirring to make a creamy batter. Do not over-mix or worry if the batter has a few lumps.

Lightly grease a heavy cast-iron griddle (or skillet) with vegetable oil. Over medium-high heat, pour ¼ cup (60 mL) of batter onto the greased griddle. As the top starts to bubble, sprinkle a handful of blueberries over each pancake. When the underside of the pancake is golden brown, flip it over using a spatula. Cook again until both sides are golden brown, for 1 to 2 minutes.

Serve immediately with a dab of butter and a drizzle of maple syrup.

Makes 14 pancakes

SPRING RECIPES

SPRING RECIPES

SPRING STARTERS

Vegan Carrot Soup VG GF

Lizzie whipped this soothing carrot soup together for dinner one night. We were all very impressed by the lovely warming effect of the spices.

3 Tbsp (45 mL) vegetable oil
1 Tbsp (15 mL) whole coriander seeds, crushed
1 Tbsp (15 mL) ground cumin
¼ **tsp (1 mL) grated whole nutmeg**
1 onion, chopped
2 garlic cloves, minced
1 lb (454 gr) carrots, chopped
1 Tbsp (15 mL) ginger root, peeled and chopped small
1 tsp (5 mL) sea salt
4 cups (1 L) Vegetable Stock with Lovage (see page 60) or 4 cups (1 L) water and
   1 tsp (5 mL) vegetable salt (see page 66)
½ **lemon, juiced**

Heat the oil and stir in spices for 2 minutes, enough to release their aromas. Add the chopped onion and sauté for 5 minutes, stirring occasionally, until the onion is soft. Add the garlic, carrots, ginger and salt, along with 4 cups (1 L) veggie stock or water and vegetable salt. Cook until the carrots are tender.

Purée in a food processor until smooth.

Add the juice of half a lemon and serve.

Makes 4 servings

Broccoli Almond Soup

This elegant soup is always a winner at dinner parties. You'll be happy to have this recipe when the overwintering sprouting broccoli produces like mad in the spring.

1 cup (250 mL) sliced almonds; reserve 1 Tbsp (15 mL) for garnish

¼ cup (60 mL) extra virgin olive oil

1 large onion, chopped

3 garlic cloves, minced

1 lb (454 gr) broccoli, stalks removed, chopped into florets

6 cups (1.5 L) water

1 dried bay leaf

6 green onions, chopped

1 tsp (5 mL) sea salt

1 tsp (5 mL) fresh-ground black pepper

2 tsp (10 mL) dried sweet basil

1 tsp (5 mL) dried sweet marjoram

1 bunch parsley, finely chopped; reserve 1 Tbsp (15 mL) for garnish

3 Tbsp (45 mL) tamari soy sauce

6 cups (1.4 L) light cream or milk or soy milk

2 Tbsp (30 mL) unbleached white flour or cornstarch or potato starch

Optional: Garnish with grated Swiss or Gruyere cheese, chopped parsley and/or toasted sliced almonds

To toast sliced almonds

Lay almond slices on a baking sheet. Place in a preheated 300F (150C) oven, turning every 5 minutes until lightly browned and evenly toasted. Set aside.

To prepare the soup

In a large saucepan, heat the oil and sauté onions and garlic together for 5 minutes until soft. Add the broccoli. Sauté over medium heat, stirring, for 10 minutes. Cover with the water. Add the bay leaf, green onions, toasted almonds (except for garnish), seasonings, parsley and soy sauce. Bring gently back to the boil. Reduce the heat.

Remove bay leaf.

Purée 2 cups (475 mL) of the soup until smooth and return the soup to the pot.

Mix the flour or non-gluten thickener with ½ cup (125 mL) of milk to form a smooth paste. Stir the rest of the milk into the saucepan, and blend the paste in. Reheat the soup, stirring as it thickens, but do not allow to boil, which makes milk soups curdle. Reduce the heat and simmer for 15 minutes for flavours to meld.

Garnish as desired and serve.

Makes 10 servings

* If you use cornstarch or potato starch for thickening, use soy milk instead of dairy, use gluten-free soy sauce and skip the optional cheese on top.

Three Sisters Soup VG* GF

'Black Turtle' beans have been grown in Mexico and Central America for more than seven thousand years. Their deep, rich flavour makes them one of the tastiest varieties of black beans grown. My planting of a 50-ft (15-m) row of this high-yielding soup bean provided 7 lb (3 kg) of shiny black beans, enough to make delicious soups, frijoles and refried-bean recipes throughout the year.

2 cups (475 mL) black beans, cooked

2 cups (475 mL) squash—delicata, butternut, pumpkin, acorn or kuri

4 Tbsp (60 mL) butter

2 large onions, thinly sliced

2 Tbsp (30 mL) garlic, minced

1 dried bay leaf

1½ tsp (7 mL) ground cumin

1½ tsp (7 mL) cayenne pepper flakes

2 tsp (10 mL) sea salt

1 tsp (5 mL) fresh-ground black pepper

4 cobs corn (475 mL), kernels removed

Optional: Garnish with sour cream and/or fresh cilantro, chopped

To cook dry beans

Wash, pick through and cover the beans with water, and leave them covered to soak overnight. Alternatively, reduce the soaking time by covering the beans with water, bringing them to the boil and turning off the heat before leaving them to soak. In either case, discard the soaking water (into the garden).

Cover the soaked beans with fresh water. Simmer for approximately 2 hours until the beans are tender but firm.

To peel squash

This task is much easier if you steam the squash over boiling water first or bake it in the oven until tender. Slice the peeled squash into ½ -inch (1-cm) chunks.

To prepare the soup

In a large saucepan, melt the butter and, stirring, sauté the onion and garlic for 5 minutes. Add the bay leaf, cumin, cayenne and salt and pepper. Sauté for another 5 minutes. Stir in the chunks of squash, corn kernels and cooked beans. Cover with water and bring to the boil. Reduce the heat and simmer for 15 minutes until the squash is tender.

Remove the bay leaf. Purée half the soup mixture and add back to the saucepan. Add enough water to achieve the desired consistency and adjust seasonings if needed. Simmer over low-medium heat for another 15 minutes.

Makes 10 servings

* if you use oil instead of butter

Spinach Salad VG* GF

This refreshing salad is chock full of vitamins and minerals, and provides a healthy tonic after the winter blahs—but tastes great anytime of the year.

2 bunches spinach, stalks removed, coarsely chopped

¼ lb (112 gr) brown mushrooms, thinly sliced

1 medium sweet onion, thinly sliced

3 eggs, hard-boiled and chopped

½ cup (125 mL) feta cheese, crumbled

Optional: Garnish with ½ cup (125 mL) dried goji berries or cranberries

Honey Dijon Dressing

½ cup (125 mL) extra virgin olive oil

¼ cup (60 mL) lemon juice

1 Tbsp (15 mL) Dijon mustard

1 Tbsp (15 mL) liquid honey

3 garlic cloves, minced

¼ tsp (1 mL) fresh-ground black pepper

Toss all the salad ingredients together, except for the berries.

Whisk the dressing together in a bowl, or shake the mixture vigorously inside a screw-top jar. Keeps refrigerated for 1 week.

Makes 4 servings

* if you leave out the feta cheese

Plant breeders have been to work so that now we can grow our own lemons on a hardy little tree that lives happily in a pot. The 'Meyer Improved' lemon (Citrus meyeri 'Improved') is a small tree with fragrant white flowers year-round, followed by thin-skinned juicy lemons. The trees are not frost-hardy, so mine spends summer outdoors and winter indoors, when I enjoy summery citrus perfume from the flowers. Water regularly to keep your lemons juicy and your lemon tree very pretty.

Kikuchi Family Sunchoke Salad VG* GF

This crunchy, refreshing salad uses ingredients readily available all winter and spring. For more sunchoke recipes and tips, see page 235.

8 oz (225 gr) sunchokes (a.k.a. Jerusalem artichokes), scrubbed and cut into thin strips

1 small carrot, cut into thin strips

½ cup (125 mL) kale leaves, cut into thin strips

Dressing

1 Tbsp (15 mL) miso

1 Tbsp (15 mL) lemon juice

1 Tbsp (15 mL) honey

1 tsp (5 mL) sesame oil

Garnish

1 Tbsp (15 mL) raw hemp hearts

Toss the sunchoke, carrot and kale strips together.

Whisk together the miso, lemon juice, honey and sesame oil.

Coat the vegetables with the dressing. Serve with hemp hearts sprinkled on top.

Makes 5 servings

* if you use maple syrup instead of honey

There are many different varieties of sunchokes (Helianthus tuberosus). They are easy to grow, spread fast, and even produce pretty yellow sunflowers in October. We consider them as versatile cold-season "potatoes" that can be dug as required.

Sprout Salad VG GF*

Pour this zingy dressing over homegrown sprouts of your choice to make a zippy salad. For advice on sprouting seeds, see page 39.

1 lb (454 gr) homegrown sprouts

Dressing
¼ cup (60 mL) extra virgin olive oil
2 tsp (10 mL) sesame oil
½ lemon, juiced
1 Tbsp (15 mL) tamari soy sauce
1 garlic clove, finely minced
¼ cup (60 mL) green onions, finely chopped
1 Tbsp (15 mL) chives, minced
2 Tbsp (30 mL) parsley, finely chopped

Topping
2 Tbsp (30 mL) gomasio (see page 39)

Whisk together all the dressing ingredients, except for the gomasio, in a bowl.

Serve the dressed sprouts with a sprinkling of gomasio to taste.

Makes 4 servings

* with gluten-free soy sauce

Jars of sprouting seeds fit easily on a windowsill when using this handy rack.

SPRING SIDE DISHES

Balsamic Glazed Parsnips and Onions VG GF

If you think you don't like parsnips, you've never tasted them prepared this way!

2 lb (908 gr) parsnips, trimmed, peeled, cut into 2 × 5-inch (5 × 12-cm) sticks

2 large white or yellow onions, peeled and quartered

Marinade

¼ cup (60 mL) extra virgin olive oil

¼ cup (60 mL) balsamic vinegar

¼ cup (60 mL) brown sugar

½ tsp (2.5 mL) sea salt

½ tsp (2.5 mL) fresh-ground black pepper

Preheat oven to 450F (230C).

In a large bowl, whisk together the marinade ingredients. Toss in the vegetables until they are well coated. Line a baking pan with a large piece of foil and transfer the marinated vegetables into the pan. Wrap them up and seal in a packet.

Bake for 25 minutes wrapped, and then open the foil, stir the vegetables, and bake opened up for 10 more minutes to give the parsnips a glazed finish.

Makes 8 servings

'Walla Walla' onions grow well from a spring seeding.

Char's Spaghetti Squash

This is one of my favourite ways of eating squash because just a few simple ingredients make it really tasty. Thanks to Tim at Santiago's Café in Victoria, BC, for sharing his mom's recipe.

2 oz (56 gr) raw cashews, roasted

2 cups (475 mL) spaghetti squash, cooked

1 tsp (5 mL) sea salt

1 tsp (5 mL) fresh-ground black pepper

½ tsp (2.5 mL) fresh-grated whole nutmeg

¼ cup (60 mL) butter

3 Tbsp (45 mL) lemon juice

3 Tbsp (45 mL) water

To roast cashews

Lay cashews on a baking pan and roast in a 300F (150C) oven, shaking every 5 minutes, until the nuts are lightly browned.

To cook the squash

Cut the spaghetti squash in half lengthwise (I use my Chinese cleaver), remove the seeds and scrape out any membrane. Season the flesh with sea salt, pepper and the grated nutmeg.

* if you use oil instead of butter

Put the squash, cut-side down, in a baking pan with a little water to just cover the pan. Bake in a 350F (175C) oven for 30 minutes or until a knife goes in easily and the flesh is al dente. Scrape the spaghetti-like strands of squash out of the skin.

In a large frying pan or skillet, sauté 2 cups (475 mL) of cooked spaghetti squash with butter, lemon juice and water for 5 to 10 minutes. Sprinkle with the roasted cashews and serve hot.

Makes 4 servings

Braised Baby Leeks   VG* GF

Baby leeks are a winter delicacy. Use them anytime you would onions—in soups, stews, pasta dishes or omelettes. We enjoy them simply braised in the oven.

12 baby leeks, green tops removed

3 Tbsp (45 mL) butter

1 cup (250 mL) Vegetable Stock with Lovage (see page 60) (or 1 vegetable stock cube)

1 tsp (5 mL) sea salt

1 tsp (5 mL) fresh-ground pepper

Preheat oven to 325F (160C).

Slice the leeks lengthwise, leaving 1 inch (2.5 cm) near the root end intact to keep them from falling apart. Wash thoroughly under running water to remove any soil.

Cut parchment paper to fit an 8-inch (20-cm) square baking dish, butter one side of the paper and set aside. Place the leeks in the baking dish, cover with stock and season with salt and pepper. Cover with the parchment paper, buttered side down. Cook for about 30 minutes, until the leeks are tender and the stock is reduced to a glaze.

Makes 3 servings

* if you use oil instead of butter

Here's a tip many people don't know. Leeks are perennial. If you slice them off just above the roots, leaving the roots in the ground, they regrow baby leeks off the base. This means that after collecting seeds, you can still harvest leeks.

Roasted Oca (New Zealand Yam) VG GF

Throughout winter we harvest New Zealand yam, or oca, directly from the garden as we need it. Oca can be cooked the same way as potatoes—boiled, baked or fried—but I like it best simply roasted. Its texture is similar to roasted carrots, with a delectable lemony flavour from the oxalic acid in the tubers.

Preheat oven to 350F (175C)

12 large oca tubers
6 garlic cloves
¼ cup (60 mL) grapeseed oil
Sprinkle of coarse sea salt
Fresh-ground pepper to taste

Throw some washed oca tubers into a garlic roaster (see page 31) or baking pan with garlic cloves. Drizzle with grapeseed oil and sprinkle with coarse sea salt and fresh-ground pepper *to taste. Bake, sizzling, for 40 to 45 minutes until tender.*

Makes 3 servings

Oxalis tuberosa is a herbaceous perennial with attractive clover-like foliage that dies back after the first hard frosts. The plant then overwinters by forming underground stem tubers. These fleshy pink tubers are known as oca or New Zealand yam, for the country in which they have become a common table vegetable. Oca is also an important staple crop of the Andean highlands, second only to the potato, due to its rapid propagation and tolerance of poor soil, high altitudes and harsh climates.

Creamed Collard Greens GF

These taste even better with a dash of hot sauce.

- **2 Tbsp (30 mL) butter**
- **1 large white or yellow onion, thinly sliced**
- **1 lb (454 gr) collard greens, stalks removed, chopped coarsely**
- **1 cup (250 mL) heavy cream**
- **½ tsp (2.5 mL) fresh-grated nutmeg**
- **1 tsp (5 mL) sea salt**

Melt the butter in a skillet over medium heat, toss in the onion and sauté gently for 10 minutes or more until caramelized. Add the chopped collard greens to the skillet, stirring for about 2 minutes until they have wilted. Reduce the heat to medium-low and stir in the cream. Simmer for about 5 minutes until the cream has reduced. Season with the nutmeg and sea salt and serve hot.

Makes 4 servings

BASIC HOT SAUCE

Wearing rubber gloves, cut the stems off a few hot peppers and blanch them in boiling white wine vinegar for 3 minutes. Put the peppers with ½ cup (125 mL) hot vinegar and 1 tsp (5 mL) of sea salt into a food processor and purée. Store in a sterilized glass sauce bottle for 3 days before consuming. The longer the sauce stands, the hotter it gets. Optional: Add sliced ginger, sugar, lime juice or minced garlic before processing.

Spring Entrées

Swiss Chard and Tomato Pizza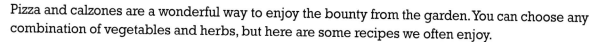

Pizza and calzones are a wonderful way to enjoy the bounty from the garden. You can choose any combination of vegetables and herbs, but here are some recipes we often enjoy.

1 batch Pizza Dough (page 123)

Topping

1 medium onion, diced

3 garlic cloves, minced

3 Tbsp (45 mL) extra virgin olive oil

4–6 oz (112–168 gr) mushrooms, sliced

6-8 dried peppers, chopped small

8 oz (225 gr) fresh tomatoes, chopped

1 tsp (5 mL) sea salt

1 tsp (5 mL) fresh-ground black pepper

1 large bunch chard greens, shredded into 2-inch (5 cm) strips

Cheese

6–8 oz (168–225 gr) grated cheese—cheddar, mozzarella, Monterey jack, soy or a blend

Preheat oven to 400F (205C).

Topping

Sauté the onions and garlic in the oil for 5 minutes until soft. Add the mushrooms, peppers and tomatoes, season with salt and pepper and sauté for another 5 minutes.

Turn off the heat and toss in the shredded chard greens until just wilted. Drain off any excess liquid.

For deep-dish pizza

Grease a 9 × 13-inch (23 × 33-cm) baking pan with 1 Tbsp (15 mL) olive oil. Spread the dough into the baking pan, and coat with 1 Tbsp (15 mL) olive oil and leave to rise in a warm room for 1 to 2 hours.

* if you use soy cheese instead of dairy

Cover with the topping and cheese.

Bake in the preheated oven for 30 minutes. TIP: If the cheese browns too fast, cover the pan with foil to complete the baking time. Check the bottom of the dough to make sure that it is cooked by tapping it to check for a "baked" feel.

For thin-crust pizza

Roll the dough out with a floured rolling pin to fit over the pizza stone or divide dough and roll into 3 small pizzas.

Spread the topping over the dough and cover with cheese(s) of your choice.

Reduce the heat in the oven to 350F (175C) and bake for up to 30 minutes.

Makes 1 large or 3 small pizzas

Pizza Dough

If you don't want to make your own, many bakeries will sell you a bag of pizza dough for a few dollars. Do give it a try, though, because it's easier than you think. This recipe makes enough for two large pizzas, and you can freeze the dough for up to three months.

1½ cups (350 mL) warm water at 115F (46C)

2 Tbsp (30 mL) sugar

2 packets (8 gr each) active dry yeast

¼ cup (60 mL) extra virgin olive oil

2 cups (475 mL) all-purpose flour, spooned and levelled,* plus more for kneading

2 cups (475 mL) whole wheat flour, spooned and levelled

1 Tbsp (15 mL) sea salt

Place the warm water and sugar in a large bowl and dissolve the sugar. Sprinkle with the yeast and leave to stand for 5 minutes until foamy. Whisk in the oil. Mix the flours and salt together, and stir into the wet ingredients using a wooden spoon, until a sticky dough forms. Turn onto a well-floured surface and bring the dough together into a ball. Punch down and knead with floured hands for about 5 minutes, until a smooth dough forms.

Brush a bowl with olive oil, and transfer the ball of dough to the oiled bowl. Turn the dough so that it gets covered by oil. Cover the bowl with a towel and leave in a warm place for about 1 hour,

*until the dough has doubled in size. Turn out onto a well-floured surface, punch down again and knead with floured hands into a smooth ball. Divide this ball into 2 or 3 sections. Roll out each section into a pizza crust using a lightly floured rolling pin. Rub the pizza stone or baking pan lightly with olive oil, and lay the crust on it, then rub it lightly with olive oil and leave to rise for another hour or so. Now it is ready to top and bake. TIP: Make sure your oven is preheated before the pizza goes in. It needs to be **hot**.*

Makes 1 large or 3 small pizzas

* Spooning the flour into the measuring cup and then scraping off the excess provides a more accurate measure than scooping directly from the bag, which compacts the flour

PIZZA STONES

If you've ever experienced soggy-bottomed pizza, consider adding a pizza stone to your kitchen. These flat ceramic disks allow you to replicate the even heat of stone baking, which makes the base crusty, and only the top juicy. The stone also works great for calzones, cookies, focaccia, bagels and other breads.

Mine came with a stainless-steel holding rack, which means I can take the baked pizza right from the oven to the table, and serve it from there, because the stone will keep the pizza hot! How much more could you ask? The stone is very absorbent, so never put it wet into a hot oven (as it will crack), and permit it to age gracefully, as it will never look as good after its first use as it did new.

Vegetable, Herb and Cheese Calzone VG*

By folding the pizza dough over the filling and crimping the outer edges together, pizza becomes a scrumptious calzone—a completely different eating experience. Use the recipe for pizza dough on page 123.

Choose one or more vegetable, herb and cheese fillings

Vegetables: Tomatoes, peppers, onions, fennel, spinach, broccoli, mushrooms, leeks, summer squash, zucchini and/or chard

Herbs: Basil, oregano and/or parsley

Cheeses: Monterey jack, mozzarella, Swiss, cheddar, fontina or soy

Preheat oven to 400F (205C).

Roll out a circle of dough and cut into 3 or 6 sections to make calzones into the size you want. Coat the dough with ½ cup (125 mL) Garden Tomato Sauce (see page 205). Cover half of each circle of dough with ½ cup (125 mL) of your choice of chopped vegetables and herbs and top with ½ cup (125 mL) of cheese(s).

* if you use soy cheese instead of dairy

Fold the empty half of the dough over the filling and crimp the edges with your fingers to make a decorative edge. Reduce the heat in the oven to 350F (175C) and bake for 30 minutes until the calzone is lightly browned. Check the bottom of the calzone to make sure that it is cooked by tapping it to check for a "baked" feel.

Makes 3 large or 6 small calzones

Jorden shows off a handful of fresh oyster mushrooms, grown from a purchased kit.

Healthy Harvest Wrap

Turn leftover salad into a delicious healthy harvest wrap by adding some grains, toasted seeds and this tangy dressing.

¼ **cup (60 mL) pumpkin seeds**

¼ **cup (60 mL) sunflower seeds**

1–2 Tbsp (15–30 mL) tamari soy sauce or Bragg Liquid Aminos

½–1 **cup (125–250 mL) of your choice of cooked grains—quinoa, brown rice, bulgur wheat or wheat berries**

½–1 **cup (125–250 mL) leftover salad**

1 multigrain wrap

Dressing

½ **cup (125 mL) olive oil**

¼ **cup (60 mL) balsamic vinegar**

2 Tbsp (30 mL) tamari soy sauce or Bragg Liquid Aminos

2 cloves garlic, minced

1 Tbsp (15 mL) liquid honey

1 tsp (5 mL) Dijon mustard

1 tsp (5 mL) black pepper

Preheat oven to 350F (190C).

In a cast-iron skillet over medium heat, stir in the seeds. When they are lightly browned, add tamari soy sauce or Bragg Liquid Aminos and sizzle for a minute or two. Remove from the heat and allow the seeds to cool.

Whisk all the dressing ingredients together.

Blend ½ to 1 cup (125 to 250 mL) of your choice of cooked grains into the same amount of leftover salad and season with a spoonful of dressing.

* *if you use maple syrup instead of honey*

** *with rice or quinoa, gluten-free soy sauce and a gluten-free wrap shell*

Lay the filling onto half of a multigrain wrap, and fold the sides in, before curling the wrap up into a roll. Place on a lightly greased baking sheet (or on parchment paper) and bake in the oven for 20 to 25 minutes until the wrap is lightly browned. Store leftover dressing in the refrigerator for another use.

Makes 1 serving and about 1 cup (250 mL) extra dressing

Morel Mushroom Omelette GF

Morels have a dark-brown, honeycombed cap and are highly regarded for their earthy flavour, which needs little embellishment. Their superb taste comes through nicely in this simple mushroom omelette.

Note that for this recipe, you need a frying pan with a handle that can go under an oven grill.

2 Tbsp (30 mL) butter

1 large onion, chopped

1 lb (454 gr) morel mushrooms, coarsely chopped

1 large sweet pepper, thinly sliced

3 large eggs

2 Tbsp (30 mL) light cream

1 tsp (5 mL) sea salt

1 tsp (5 mL) fresh-ground black pepper

10 fresh basil leaves, chopped

1 cup (250 mL) fresh-grated cheese—cheddar, Swiss, fontina, Parmigiano-Reggiano

Preheat oven to 400F (205C).

Sauté the onion in the butter for 5 minutes until it has softened. Add the mushrooms and pepper and sauté for another 5 minutes.

Whisk the eggs with the cream and the seasonings and pour over the sautéed vegetables in the frying pan. Cook the base of the omelette over medium heat for about 5 minutes without browning it, which will affect flavour.

Top with fresh basil leaves and cover with the grated cheese. Place the frying pan 6 inches (15 cm) below a preheated oven grill. In a few minutes the top will have risen fluffily and be lightly browned.

TIP: Have everyone ready to eat because ideally this dish should be served immediately!

Makes 4 servings

Asparagus, Mushroom and Fontina Quiche

This is one of my favourite fillings for a quiche, but feel free to change the cheese to Swiss or extra-old cheddar if you prefer.

Pastry

½ batch No-Fail Shortcrust Pastry, next page, rolled to fit a 10-inch (24-cm) quiche dish, chilled in the refrigerator until needed

Filling

2 Tbsp (30 mL) olive oil

1 onion, chopped

6 asparagus spears, chopped into 1-inch (2.5-cm) pieces

4 oz (112 g) mushrooms, sliced

8 oz (225 gr) fontina cheese, grated

Custard

5 large or 6 medium eggs

1 cup (250 mL) light cream

Pinch lemon zest

2 Tbsp (30 mL) flour

½ tsp (2.5 mL) salt

½ tsp (2.5 mL) fresh-ground pepper

Preheat oven to 400F (205C).

Sauté the vegetables in the olive oil for 5 minutes and layer into the quiche dish. Cover with the fontina cheese.

In a food processor, blend the custard ingredients until smooth, and pour the custard over the filling in the dish.

Reduce the oven to 350F (175C) and bake on the middle shelf for 25 minutes. To prevent excess browning, cover the dish with foil and bake for another 20 minutes until the centre has set and is firm to the touch. Leave to cool for 10 minutes before serving.

Makes 6 servings

If you are inclined toward self-sufficiency, I heartily recommend a flock of feathery friends for zero-mile eggs. Check your local bylaws on backyard poultry. As long as you don't drive your neighbours mad with a rooster that crows at four in the morning and you look after your "girls" properly, there's no reason for neighbours to complain. If they do, just give them a dozen eggs!

No-Fail Shortcrust Pastry

Some people shudder at the thought of having to make pastry from scratch, so I am including instructions on how to make perfect shortcrust pastry, step by step. Once mastered, this pastry opens the door to preparing wonderful fruit pies and quiches using the garden harvest. This recipe is enough for two quiches, or one quiche with fruit pie for dessert.

2½ cups (600 mL) unbleached white flour (or substitute half white flour and half whole wheat flour)
Pinch of sea salt
1 cup (250 mL) chilled butter (or substitute half butter and half vegetable shortening), cut into large pieces
1 large egg (or 2 small ones)
½ cup (125 mL) cold water

1. *In a large mixing bowl, blend the flour and salt, and cut in the butter using 2 knives or a pastry cutter, until a coarse crumble forms.*

   Beat 1 large egg (or 2 small eggs) in a measuring cup and top up to ½ cup (125 mL) with cold water.

2. *Pour the egg liquid over the crumble, and use a fork to gently bring the mixture together into a loose ball. If too wet, dust with a little more flour. If too dry, add a few more drops of cold water until the dough begins to hold together. Handle the pastry as little as possible, and add the minimum amount of liquid, to keep the crust flaky when baked.*

3. *Use your hands to bring the ball of pastry firmly together and place onto a lightly floured surface. Cut in half. TIP: If you only need 1 quiche or pie, wrap the remaining pastry ball in wax paper and leave it refrigerated for a few days until you need it, or freeze it in a bag for later.*

4. *Dust a surface and a rolling pin lightly with flour. Slightly flatten the ball of pastry onto the floured surface with the rolling pin, and start rolling, always outward from the centre, aiming for a circle of even thickness.*

5. *When the circle of pastry is large enough to fit your quiche dish, fold it over the rolling pin, and unfold it over the dish, so that it settles comfortably inside, leaving at least a 1-inch (2.5-cm) rim to flop over the edge. TIP: If the rim is too large, use scissors to cut it back to a 1-inch (2.5-cm) width all the way around. Fold the excess pastry underneath, so that it forms a smooth edge. Make a decorative wavy edge all the way around, using your thumb and forefinger of one hand, and crimping with your forefinger of the other hand. Put the pastry-lined quiche/pie dish in the refrigerator to chill while preparing the rest of the ingredients.*

Makes two 10-inch (24-cm) single crusts, or one covered pie

Santiago's Polenta Wedges

Serve these tasty polenta wedges hot or cold with black beans, salsa and/or a dollop of sour cream. If you like, brush the wedges with olive oil and lightly grill them on the barbecue.

TIP: Choose a large pot with high sides because polenta spits as it cooks!

2 Tbsp (60 mL) dried tomatoes, chopped (see **Dehydrator, page 27**)

¼ cup (60 mL) dried peppers or ½ cup (125 mL) fresh peppers, finely chopped

3 large garlic cloves

3 Tbsp (45 mL) vegetable oil

1 cup (250 mL) red onions, diced

½ tsp (2.5 mL) dried red chilies, crushed

½ tsp (2.5 mL) dried oregano

½ tsp (2.5 mL) dried basil

1 tsp (5 mL) sea salt

1 tsp (5 mL) black pepper

3 cups (700 mL) Vegetable Stock with Lovage (see page 60)

1 cup (250 mL) tomato juice (juice using a stovetop steamer, page 27)

1 cup (250 mL) corn kernels

1½ cup (350 mL) coarse cornmeal

Throw the dried tomatoes, dried peppers (if using) and garlic cloves into a food processor and whiz into small pieces.

Heat the oil in the cooking pot, and sauté the onions, fresh peppers (if using), chilies, oregano, basil, salt and black pepper with the whizzed mixture, until the onions are soft.

Add the veggie stock, tomato juice and corn kernels and bring to the boil. Slowly add the cornmeal, whisking constantly. Reduce the heat, and cook for approximately 10 minutes, until the polenta has thickened and comes off the side of the pot.

Pour the polenta onto a baking sheet, spreading to about 1 inch (2.5 cm) thick. Leave to cool.

Cut into 4-inch (10-cm) squares, and store refrigerated, placed between sheets of waxed paper in a sealed glass container. To serve as polenta wedges, cut the squares in half.

Polenta will store well for up to a week.

Makes 12 to 18 polenta wedges

Basic Garden Polenta VG* GF

Polenta is made from cornmeal and tastes wonderful in combination with tomato sauce, black beans and tangy aged cheese, as well as with sautéed vegetables such as zucchini, green onions and peppers, and herbs such as sage, thyme, oregano, basil and parsley.

- **1 cup (250 mL) yellow cornmeal**
- **4 cups (1 L) water**
- **1 tsp (5 mL) salt**
- **2 Tbsp (60 mL) butter or olive oil**
- **1 tsp (5 mL) dried Greek oregano**
- **½ cup (125 mL) Parmigiano-Reggiano cheese**
- **½ tsp (2.5 mL) fresh-ground black pepper**

In a small bowl, combine the cornmeal and 1 cup (250 mL) of the water. Bring the remaining 3 cups (700 mL) of water to the boil and pour in the moistened cornmeal, whisking constantly so that it does not turn lumpy. Cook over a low heat until smooth and thickened. Remove from the heat and leave to sit for 5 minutes.

Stir in the butter or oil, oregano, Parmigiano-Reggiano and pepper.

Makes 4 servings

* if you leave out the cheese and use olive oil instead of butter

Spring Stir-Fry `VG*` `GF**`

Get your wok out and prepare the freshest fast food ever! The secret to stir-frying is starting with the oil hot, and tossing the ingredients over very high heat until just tender and still crunchy. Serve this recipe by itself or together with quinoa, rice or noodles.

Sauce

½ cup (125 mL) orange juice

2 Tbsp (30 mL) tamari soy sauce

1 Tbsp (15 mL) honey

1 Tbsp (15 mL) fresh-grated ginger

2 garlic cloves, minced

2 tsp (10 mL) sesame oil

1 Tbsp (15 mL) cornstarch

Stir-Fry

3 Tbsp (45 mL) vegetable oil—peanut or grapeseed

8 oz (225 gr) firm tofu, cut into 1-inch (2.5-cm) cubes

1 cup (250 mL) sliced carrots

1 lb (454 gr) snow peas or sugar snap peas, with strings removed

1 bunch green onions, chopped

2 bunches of spring greens, shredded—collards, spinach, cabbage or kale

1 bunch garlic scapes, chopped (optional)

Sauce

Mix all the above ingredients together, except the cornstarch.

Put the cornstarch in a small bowl with a few spoonfuls of the sauce, and stir until smooth. Stir back into the sauce so that it thickens as it cooks.

Stir-Fry

Heat the oil, add the tofu and turn it a few times until it is golden. Remove the tofu from the oil using a slotted spoon. Stir-fry the carrots until mostly tender, then add the peas, green onions and garlic scapes, if used. Add the shredded greens and toss them quickly until they wilt. Add the sauce to the wok, stir-frying for a few more minutes until the vegetables are coated.

Makes 4 servings

* if you use maple syrup instead of honey

** with gluten-free soy sauce

Opposite: Spring broccoli and snow peas, perfect for a stir-fry.

Lentils with Cabbage   VG GF

This recipe is delicious with grains such as quinoa or rice.

1 cup (250 mL) red or green split lentils, picked over, washed and drained

4 cups (1 L) water

½ tsp (2.5 mL) turmeric

¼ cup (60 mL) vegetable oil

1 tsp (5 mL) cumin seeds

5 cloves garlic, minced

½ onion, sliced finely

8 oz (225 gr) cabbage, cored and shredded finely

2 fresh hot chilies, or 1 tsp (5 mL) dried chilies, chopped

1½ tsp (7 mL) sea salt

½ cup (125 mL) Garden Tomato Sauce (see page 205)

½ tsp (2.5 mL) finely grated ginger root

Put the lentils and water into a heavy saucepan and bring to the boil, removing any scum that may come to the top. Add the turmeric and stir to blend in. Cover the pan, and leaving the lid slightly ajar, turn the heat to low and simmer for 1 hour.

While the lentils are cooking, heat the oil in a frying pan, and add the cumin seeds, allowing them to sizzle for a few seconds. Add the garlic, then the onion, cabbage and chilies, stirring and frying for about 10 minutes, until the cabbage is slightly crunchy and browned. Add ¼ tsp (1 mL) sea salt and turn the heat off under the frying pan.

To the cooked lentils add the remaining 1¼ tsp (6 mL) sea salt, tomato sauce and grated ginger. Cover and cook for another 10 minutes. Just before serving, stir in the cabbage mixture and simmer for 5 minutes until the cabbage mixture has heated through.

Makes 4 servings

Pasta with Camille's Nettle Pesto

Choose your favourite pasta to enjoy with this pesto. Nettle pesto can be sealed in a glass container and refrigerated for up to a week, or can be frozen for future use. This is a delicious way of getting a spring tonic into your system anytime you want it. Thanks to Camille's restaurant in Victoria, BC, for the recipe.

3 lb (1.4 kg) fresh nettle tips (before plants go to seed)

½–1 cup (125–250 mL) extra virgin olive oil

1 cup (250 mL) sunflower seeds, hazelnuts, or pine nuts

12 garlic cloves

1 cup (250 mL) Parmigiano-Reggiano cheese, shredded

1 lemon, juice and zest

Sea salt to taste

Wearing gloves, harvest the tender tips of new-growth nettles. Fill a large basin with cold water and, using tongs, wash the greens. Put washed greens into a large pot of boiling water and blanch them for 30 seconds. Using tongs, remove the greens from the hot water and cool them down fast in a large bowl of ice water. Drain in a colander and squeeze as dry as possible.

Place the oil, nuts and garlic into a small pot on medium heat. Watch carefully and remove from the heat when the nuts are golden brown and the garlic is softened. Remove the nuts and garlic from the oil and leave oil to cool.

Put the nettles, nuts, garlic, Parmigiano-Reggiano, salt and lemon into the bowl of a food processor. Pulse a few times to blend. With the blade turning slowly, drizzle in the oil, until you reach the desired consistency for your pesto. You may not need all the oil; retain any extra for salad dressing.

Makes 3½ cups (825 mL)

* with gluten-free pasta choice

SPRING DESSERTS

Strawberry Rhubarb Loaf

This refreshing and moist loaf tastes even more divine with a touch of Cream-Cheese Frosting (see page 244).

⅓ **cup (80 mL) vegetable oil—grapeseed or sunflower**

¾ **cup (180 mL) light brown sugar, packed**

1 egg, beaten

¼ **cup (60 mL) sour cream**

½ **tsp (2.5 mL) pure vanilla extract**

1 Tbsp (15 mL) rum (optional)

1 cup (250 mL) whole wheat flour

½ **tsp (2.5 mL) sea salt**

1 tsp (5 mL) baking soda

1 cup (250 mL) rhubarb, diced

½ **cup (125 mL) strawberries, sliced (drain any excess juices and retain for another use)**

¼ **cup (60 mL) currants (optional)**

Preheat the oven to 350F (175C).

In a medium bowl, beat the oil and the sugar together to a smooth consistency. Add the egg and stir in the sour cream, vanilla extract, and rum if you are tippling! Beat wet ingredients together until smooth.

In a small bowl, sift the flour, salt and baking soda together. Using a wooden spoon, gradually blend the dry ingredients into the wet ingredients until a smooth batter is formed.

Fold the rhubarb, strawberries and currants into the batter without mixing the fruit to a mush.

Using a spatula, spread the batter into a parchment-lined or greased 9 × 5-inch (23 × 13-cm) loaf pan. Bake it in the centre of the preheated oven for 45 minutes, when a wooden toothpick inserted in the middle should come out clean. Leave the pan to cool on a baking rack for 10 minutes.

Score around the edges before inverting and tapping the loaf out of the pan. Leave to completely cool on a baking rack before storing in a cake tin.

Makes one 9 × 5-inch (23 × 13-cm) loaf

Stewed Rhubarb VG GF

The first fruit of the season is simply divine when gently simmered and served with a dollop of yogourt and a sprinkle of granola (see Jeanie's Honey Granola, page 18).

8–10 stalks rhubarb, washed and chopped into ½-inch (1-cm) chunks

1 orange, peel and juice

½ cup (125 mL) raw cane sugar

2 sprigs sweet cicely leaves (allows you to cut back on sugar)

¼ cup (60 mL) currants or raisins

2 chunks candied ginger, finely chopped (optional)

½ tsp (2.5 mL) ground cinnamon

Put the rhubarb and the orange juice in a saucepan and slowly bring to a gentle simmer while stirring.

Stir in the sugar, sweet cicely, dried fruit, ginger and cinnamon powder and simmer gently until the rhubarb is just soft.

Remove from the heat and allow to cool.

Garnish with grated orange peel.

Makes 6 servings

This attractive perennial is one of the earliest crops in the garden. Rhubarb is a heavy feeder and loves a mulch of manure every year. The woody clumps need to be divided every few years to get the best production, which is when an axe works wonders! Once the weather warms up, it's best to stop harvesting, as oxalic acid builds up in the plants and it's good to leave some leaves to feed the roots for next year's crop.

Apple Maple Cobbler

The perfect combination of apples and maple syrup makes this dessert s'more-ish. Best enjoyed still warm with a dollop of something creamy!

4 large apples peeled, cored and sliced (see Apple Peeler, page 32)

½ tsp (2.5 mL) cinnamon powder

1 cup (250 mL) maple syrup

2 eggs, beaten

3 Tbsp (45 mL) unsalted butter, melted

1 tsp (5 mL) pure vanilla extract

2 tsp (10 mL) fresh-squeezed lemon juice

½ cup (125 mL) whole wheat flour

1 tsp (5 mL) baking powder

Preheat the oven to 375F (190C).

Butter a 9 × 13-inch (23 × 33-cm) glass baking dish.

Toss the apples with cinnamon and ½ cup (125 mL) maple syrup, and scoop into greased baking dish.

Whisk the eggs with the melted butter, vanilla, ½ cup (125 mL) maple syrup and the lemon juice.

Sift the flour and baking powder together.

Blend the wet and dry ingredients until a smooth batter forms. Using a spatula, smooth the batter over the apples in the baking dish.

Turn the oven down to 350F (175C) and bake for 30 minutes, until the top of the cobbler has risen and is lightly browned.

Makes 8 to 10 servings

'Jonagold' is one of my favourite apple varieties. Very productive, crisp and juicy, it is a late variety that stores well. Early July is the time to thin apple trees, which drop fruit automatically but not enough to ensure energy for good-sized fruit. To check that apples are ripe, lift the fruit in your palm and give a slight twist. If ripe, the apple should come away from the tree easily. Apple trees need pruning yearly to encourage new growth and maintain a strong framework.

Carrot Cake for a Crowd

I've tried many versions of carrot cake but this recipe gets the star! It's moist and fruity with loads of ingredients that make it irresistible on the first bite. For a more decadent cake, double the quantity of frosting and split the cake horizontally, adding a sandwich layer of icing in the middle. This is a large cake, suitable for a party, but it also freezes well.

5 cups (1.2 L) whole wheat flour (or half whole wheat and half unbleached white)

1½ tsp (7 mL) sea salt

1 tsp (5 mL) ground cinnamon

1 tsp (5 mL) fresh-grated nutmeg

2 tsp (10 mL) baking soda

2 tsp (10 mL) baking powder

4 eggs

1 cup (250 mL) grapeseed oil

1½ cups (350 mL) light liquid honey

4 cups (1 L) grated carrots

½ cup (125 mL) pineapple tidbits, reserving a few for an optional garnish

½ cup (125 mL) hazelnuts (or walnuts), toasted and chopped; reserve a few for garnish

1 cup (250 mL) dried raisins soaked in 1 cup (250 mL) boiling water (or substitute half the water for sherry)

1 batch Cream Cheese Frosting (see opposite page)

½ cup (125 mL) shredded coconut (optional)

Preheat oven to 350F (175C).

In a large bowl, sift together the flour(s), salt, spices and leavening agents. In a second large bowl, beat the eggs and slowly drizzle in the oil and then the honey, beating to emulsify. Add the dry ingredients gradually to the wet ingredients, beating well to mix together.

Using a wooden spoon, stir in the grated carrots, pineapple, nuts, the dried fruit and its soaking liquid and coconut, if using. Mix well.

Using a spatula, scrape the batter into a 9 × 15-inch (23 × 38-cm) greased baking pan with high sides (or for 2 smaller cakes, use 8-inch/ 20-cm square or round cake pans). Bake in the preheated oven for 50 minutes to 1 hour. If the top browns too much, cover with foil to complete the baking time. Test with a toothpick in the centre to make sure the cake is properly cooked. Allow to cool before frosting.

Spread frosting over the cake, and add as a sandwich layer if desired. For a nice touch, garnish the frosted cake with chopped, toasted nuts, pineapple chunks or coconut sprinkles.

Makes 18 to 20 servings

Cream Cheese Frosting

8 oz (225 gr) cream cheese, at room temperature
½ cup (125 mL) butter, at room temperature
½ cup (125 mL) light liquid honey
1 tsp (5 mL) pure vanilla extract

Beat the cream cheese, butter, honey and vanilla until smooth and creamy.

Makes about 1½ cups (350 mL)

Rumpot VG GF

Rumpot is a traditional German way of preserving fruits grown throughout the year. You can start making rumpot from the first fruit harvest of the season to the last harvest of fall. Thanks to my friend Thomas from Switzerland for this recipe—even though I almost got drunk at breakfast!

1 part sugar
2 parts mix of firm ripe seasonal fruits—strawberries, currants, blueberries, gooseberries, plums, cherries, pears, grapes, peaches and nectarines
Rum, 26% alcohol or 52 proof

Clean and sterilize a 1-gallon (4-L) glass jar with a well-fitting lid. Wash the fruit and cut it into bite-sized pieces. Weigh the fruit and add half of its weight in sugar. Just cover the fruit with rum.

Continue to add layers of fruit as it comes into season, adding half the weight in sugar and covering it with rum. It's important that the fruit is always covered with rum. Set aside in a cool, dark place.

After adding the last layer of fruit, or when the jar is completely full, leave to stand for 6 weeks.

Makes one 1-gallon (4-L) jar

Spring Drinks

Fruit Smoothies VG* GF

Fruit smoothies are a great way to enjoy summer year-round. They are quick and easy to make if you have a blender with a good motor, along with lots of frozen fruit in the freezer.

1 banana, fresh or frozen
1 cup (250 mL) apple juice (or yogourt)
1 cup (250 mL) frozen raspberries, strawberries, blackcurrants, blueberries,
   blackberries or saskatoon berries
¼ cup (60 mL) liquid honey or maple syrup (optional)

Throw into the blender and blend until smooth. Add more apple juice if too thick.

Makes 2 servings

* if you use maple syrup and apple juice

Jackie's Green Smoothie VG GF

Try this nutritious green smoothie—you'll be amazed how delicious it is! Toss in seasonal fruit when available—a peach or pear makes it even better. In summer, make it even more zero-mile by thickening the smoothie with a cup of raw zucchini instead of the banana.

4 packed cups (1 L) raw greens like kale, spinach, lettuce, chard, coarsely chopped, stems removed
1 cup (250 mL) apples, fresh or frozen, cored and chopped
1 banana, fresh or frozen, chopped
½ cup (125 mL) apple juice
½ **cup (125 mL) water or more, depending on your preferred thickness**
Juice of 2 lemons
1 tsp (5 mL) ground cinnamon
A few ice cubes (optional)

Blend the ingredients together, then enjoy this healthy pick-me-up!

Makes 2 servings

SUMMER

SUMMER RECIPES

Summer Starters

Minty Hummus VG GF

Hummus is a chickpea pâté that is rich and spicy and full of protein. This minty version is wonderful to have around in summer. It can be enjoyed as a dip for raw vegetable sticks or triangles of pita bread, put in grilled panini or focaccia sandwiches, and spread over wraps before they are filled. Make it a day ahead of serving to allow the flavours to meld.

1 cup (250 mL) garbanzo beans (chickpeas), cooked

¼ cup (60 mL) cooking liquid leftover from beans, or water

3 medium garlic cloves, chopped coarsely

1 lime, juiced

½ cup (125 mL) sesame tahini

1 tsp (5 mL) sea salt

½ tsp (2.5 mL) fresh-ground pepper

½ tsp (2.5 mL) ground cumin

½ tsp (2.5 mL) ground coriander

½ tsp (2.5 mL) chili powder

3 Tbsp (45 mL) fresh mint leaves (or 1 Tbsp/15 mL dried mint)

Purée all ingredients in a food processor to your desired consistency—smooth or slightly chunkier if you prefer.

Store in the refrigerator.

Makes 1½ cups (350 mL)

Beet Hummus VG GF

A colourful and tasty combination, beets, chickpeas and garlic are harvested from the garden for an eye-catching topping on cucumber rounds or crackers. Or just scoop it up with endive leaves or sticks of carrots, peppers and celery.

4 medium beets

1 cup (250 mL) chickpeas (garbanzo beans), cooked and drained

4 Tbsp (60 mL) sesame tahini

2 garlic cloves, chopped

1 Tbsp (15 mL) ground cumin

2 lemons, juiced

1 tsp (5 mL) sea salt

½ tsp (2.5 mL) fresh-ground pepper to taste

In a medium lidded saucepan, cover beets with water and simmer for about 30 minutes, testing with a knife for tenderness. Cool and peel, then cut into quarters.

Place all the ingredients in a food processor and pulse until smooth. Taste and adjust the seasonings as desired.

Chill before serving and keep refrigerated.

Makes 2 cups (475 mL)

It's hard to believe you can grow chickpeas in your own backyard. The attractive foliage with pretty pink flowers makes a great low groundcover. There are only two chickpeas in every pod, so you need to sow a long row for enough to harvest for eating.

Garlic Scape Pesto VG GF

I can't resist the flavour of garlic from the early-summer scapes. They provide a delicious pungent addition to this pesto recipe, which is then included in many other dishes.

- **2 cups (475 mL) garlic scapes (stems only), cut into ½-inch (1-cm) pieces**
- **3 Tbsp (45 mL) sunflower seeds, toasted**
- **3 cups (700 mL) fresh basil leaves, loosely packed**
- **½ tsp (2.5 mL) sea salt**
- **½ tsp (2.5 mL) fresh-ground black pepper**
- **½ cup (125 mL) extra virgin olive oil**

Place all the ingredients in a food processor except for the oil. Pulse until well blended, and then slowly pour in the olive oil through the spout to reach a smooth, thick consistency.

Keep refrigerated. Can also be frozen in 1-cup (250-mL) containers for later use.

Makes 3 cups (700 mL)

Mint Tzatziki VG* GF

This tangy Greek condiment goes perfectly with so many dishes—I can never get enough of it on hot sunny days!

- **2 cups (475 mL) cucumber, grated**
- **1 tsp (5 mL) sea salt**
- **1 cup (250 mL) plain Greek yogourt**
- **2 Tbsp (30 mL) fresh mint, finely chopped**
- **1 garlic clove, minced**
- **½ lemon, zest and juice**

Put the cucumber into a shallow bowl and sprinkle with the salt. Leave to stand. The cucumber will sweat.

With clean hands, squeeze the liquid out of the cucumber before adding the rest of the ingredients.

Cover and refrigerate until needed. Keeps well refrigerated for several days.

Makes 1½ cups (350 mL)

* if you use soy yogourt

Potted Wild Salmon GF

This dish is ideal for picnics, as a spread on crackers or as a raw veggie dip.

1 cup (250 mL) white wine

1 bay leaf, dried

6 peppercorns

½ tsp (2.5 mL) grated nutmeg

1 tsp (5 mL) salt

1 tsp (5 mL) pepper

8 oz (225 gr) wild salmon fillet

½ cup (125 mL) sour cream

2 Tbsp (30 mL) mint leaves, minced

2 Tbsp (30 mL) lemon juice

In a small saucepan, combine the wine, bay leaf, peppercorns, nutmeg, salt and pepper. Simmer for 5 minutes.

Add the salmon, cover and poach for 10 minutes.

Drain the salmon and cool, reserving the cooking liquid. Reduce the cooking liquid over medium heat until only 2 Tbsp (30 mL) of the liquid remain. Remove any skin and bones from the salmon, along with the bay leaf, and put the salmon meat in a food processor. Add 2 Tbsp (30 mL) of the reduced liquid and the rest of the ingredients, and process in several pulses until well mixed. Check for seasoning and transfer to a crock. Cover and chill for several hours.

TIP: Remove from the refrigerator 30 minutes before serving.

Makes 4 to 6 servings

Opposite: You may regret planting mint in the garden as it takes over fast! It's best to grow mint in planters and keep them handy to the kitchen for harvest. Mint is refreshing in cold summer drinks, is wonderful boiled with baby potatoes and adds a cool kick to summer salads.

Corn and Bean Salsa VG GF

This traditional combination of complementary proteins—corn and beans—makes a tangy salsa to go with burgers, a dip with chips or a tasty filling in taco shells.

6 yellow and 6 red tomatoes, chopped into small pieces

1 small sweet onion or 3 green onions, finely chopped

½ bunch cilantro, finely minced

1 corn cob, kernels removed

8 oz (225 gr) black beans, cooked

2 large red peppers, roasted and diced small (see Marinated Roasted Peppers, page 82)

1½ limes, juiced

1 tsp (5 mL) coarse salt

Mix all the above ingredients together and leave to marinate for several hours.

Makes 2 cups (475 mL)

Sweet red peppers in the greenhouse.

Summer Greens Salad Dressing

It's not only about vibrant fresh greens when it comes to summer salads, but also what you dress them with. So here's one of my favourite dressings for a just-harvested summer salad. For summer salads, we harvest arugula, lettuce, parcel, spinach, kale, chard, chicory, endive, cilantro, cress and a whole bunch of tasty herbs.

- **1 cup (250 mL) extra virgin olive oil**
- **⅓ cup (80 mL) red wine vinegar**
- **2 Tbsp (30 mL) balsamic vinegar**
- **1 Tbsp (15 mL) soy sauce**
- **1 tsp (5 mL) Dijon mustard**
- **1 Tbsp (15 mL) honey**
- **3 Tbsp (45 mL) sesame seeds, toasted**
- **1 tsp (5 mL) salt**
- **1 tsp (5 mL) black pepper**

Whisk all the ingredients or whirl together in a blender until well mixed.

Give the dressing a good shake, then right before serving, pour over the greens and toss. TIP: Go easy when pouring—a few tablespoonfuls are often enough, and soggy salads are not appealing!

Store extra dressing in the refrigerator for use as needed.

Makes 1½ cups (350 mL)

*with maple syrup instead of honey

**with gluten-free soy sauce

Summer Tomato Salsa

This salsa is fast and easy to make, and so handy to have around as a condiment for many recipes. Serving early-evening drinks in the garden, with a bowlful of chips and salsa, is my favourite thing to do in summer.

12 large tomatoes, chopped into quarters

1 lb (454 gr) red pepper, coarsely chopped

1 lb (454 gr) red onion, coarsely chopped

2 jalapeno peppers, coarsely chopped (TIP: leave seeds in for a more piquant salsa)

3 cloves garlic, quartered

1½ cups (350 mL) apple cider vinegar

3 cups (700 mL) water

1 cup (250 mL) dark brown sugar, lightly packed

1 cup (250 mL) fresh cilantro, finely chopped

In a food processor, combine all the vegetables, except for the cilantro, and pulse until well chopped but not mushy.

Put into saucepan, add the vinegar, water and sugar, and slowly bring to the boil. Reduce heat

and simmer for 10 minutes, until the vegetables have softened.

Add the cilantro and simmer for 1 minute.

Allow to chill before serving. Keep refrigerated.

Makes 6 cups (1.4 L)

There are many ways to extend the season of enjoyment by preserving your homegrown tomato harvest—drying, freezing, salsa, soups, sauces and paste.

To preserve bumper tomato harvests, I divide them into type:

Cherry: Small round fruits, good for early harvests and short-season summers

Salad: Uniformly round, firm 2-inch (5-cm) tomatoes that can be cut into quarters, tossed into salads or enjoyed fresh

Paste: Large meaty tomatoes with few seeds, good for cooking into soups, sauces and paste

Beefsteak: Good eaten fresh, 3-inch (7.5-cm) and larger, round, ribbed or heart-shaped, and late to ripen

Novelty: In all colours, shapes and sizes—beautiful eaten fresh and delicious slow-roasted

Potato, Mint and Pea Salad

It's fun grabbling for tender baby potatoes under the plant, without disturbing the rest of the crop. In hot summers, this is one of my favourite refreshing and cooling salads.

Dressing

½ cup (125 mL) mayonnaise (see Free-Range Egg Mayonnaise, page 157)

1 tsp (5 mL) prepared Dijon mustard

1 tsp (5 mL) sea salt

1 tsp (5 mL) fresh-grated black pepper

Salad

2 lb (900 gr) red or white baby potatoes, cooked, chilled and cubed

1 cup (250 mL) shelled peas, cooked

½ cucumber, diced

5 sprigs fresh mint, finely chopped

1 bunch chives, finely chopped

½ medium sweet onion, diced small

1 tsp (5 mL) nasturtium capers (see following recipe) or pickled peppercorns (optional)

Blend the dressing ingredients together, and then toss with the rest of the ingredients.

Chill in the refrigerator until ready to serve.

Makes 6 to 8 servings

Nasturtium Capers

2 Tbsp (30 mL) pickling salt

1 cup (250 mL) water

½ cup (125 mL) nasturtium seed pods (use young pods that are still green and soft)

¾ cup (180 mL) white wine vinegar

2 tsp (10 mL) sugar

1 dried bay leaf

2 sprigs fresh thyme

Bring the salt and water to a boil in a small saucepan. Put the nasturtium seed pods in a 1-cup (250-mL) glass jar and pour the boiling brine over them. Cover and let soak at room temperature for 3 days. Drain the seed pods.

Bring the vinegar, sugar, bay leaf and thyme to a boil. Pour over the seed pods and let cool. Cover the jar and refrigerate for 3 days before using. Keeps 6 months refrigerated.

Cinco de Mayo Slaw

Cooling and crunchy, this is the perfect salad for al fresco eating and picnics. In summer I often whip this recipe together, because it keeps well refrigerated and is handy to have around.

- 2 cups (475 mL) red cabbage, finely shredded
- 1 cup (250 mL) green cabbage, finely shredded
- 2 green onions, chopped
- 3 Tbsp (45 mL) fresh cilantro or parsley leaves, chopped
- ½ cup (125 mL) mayonnaise (see Free-Range Egg Mayonnaise, below)
- 2 tsp (10 mL) sea salt
- 2 Tbsp (30 mL) lime juice
- 2 tsp (10 mL) honey
- Pinch of cayenne pepper, powdered

Combine all the ingredients, toss well and chill before serving.

This slaw stores well refrigerated for a week.

Makes 4 to 6 servings

Free-Range Egg Mayonnaise GF

Thanks to our backyard chickens, we enjoy this fresh-tasting mayonnaise with sandwiches and for dishes like Cinco de Mayo Slaw. You can use a food processor or a blender to mix it up, or a good wire whisk for a bit of a workout. The secret to making creamy, thick mayonnaise emulsion is to add the oil very slowly, drizzling it in a bit at a time. Homemade mayonnaise does not keep as long as store-bought because it does not contain preservatives, but it is far superior in taste.

- 6 eggs, yolks only (TIP: Use cold eggs only)
- 1½ tsp (7 mL) prepared mustard
- 1½ tsp (7 mL) Worcestershire sauce
- ¼ tsp (1 mL) cayenne pepper
- 5 cups (1.2 L) grapeseed or olive oil
- ¾ cup (180 mL) white wine vinegar
- ¼ cup (60 mL) lemon juice

Beat the egg yolks and seasonings together until smooth.

Blend the oil, vinegar and lemon juice together.

Slowly drizzle the oil mixture into the egg mixture until a smooth, thick emulsion forms, et voilà— homemade mayonnaise!

Keeps in the refrigerator for up to a week.

Makes one ½-gallon (2 L) jar

Tangy Greek Salad GF

This is one of my favourite summer salads—fast to put together and so refreshing.

2 medium tomatoes, chopped
1 large bell pepper, seeded and chopped
½ cucumber, seeded and chopped
½ red onion, chopped
12–15 kalamata olives, drained
6 oz (170 gr) feta cheese, crumbled into chunks

Dressing
2 Tbsp (30 mL) lemon juice
1 tsp (5 mL) fresh oregano leaves or ½ tsp (2.5 mL) dried
¼ cup (60 mL) olive oil, extra virgin, cold pressed
Salt and fresh-ground pepper to taste

Chop the vegetables into roughly the same-sized pieces and add the olives.

Combine the dressing ingredients in a small bowl and whisk until well blended. Toss the dressing with the vegetables.

Refrigerate for a few hours before serving.

Just before serving, sprinkle the feta cheese over the salad.

Makes 4 servings

Fresh Mint Tabouleh

This refreshing summer salad makes great picnic food. It's also delicious eaten together with hummus and tzatziki inside a wrap.

If using bulgur wheat

2¼ cups (535 mL) dry bulgur wheat, rinsed

3 cups (700 mL) boiling water

1 tsp (5 mL) sea salt

Combine the bulgur, water and salt in a bowl.   *Cover the bowl and let stand for 1 hour or until all the water is absorbed and the bulgur is chewable.*

If using quinoa

2 cups (475 mL) quinoa, well rinsed

4 cups (1 L) water

Bring the grains and the water to a boil, turn down the heat to very low and put the lid on the saucepan. Simmer for 15 minutes and then   *remove from the stovetop. Leave the lid on for another 10 minutes and lift off to fluffy perfection!*

Vegetables and dressing

½ cup (125 mL) lemon or lime juice

½ cup (125 mL) extra virgin olive oil

1 tsp (5 mL) garlic, finely minced

½ cup (125 mL) fresh parsley, minced

½ cup (125 mL) fresh mint, finely chopped or 3 tsp (15 mL) dried mint

¼ cup (60 mL) scallions or onions, finely chopped

2 large tomatoes, diced small

Toss the bulgur or the quinoa with the dressing. Refrigerate for 2 to 3 hours before serving. Garnish with the diced tomatoes just before serving.

Makes 6 to 8 servings

* if you use quinoa for the grain

Summer Entrées

Zucchini, Red Pepper and Feta Quiche

Here's another winning combination of ingredients for a tasty quiche that "real men" will definitely eat!

Pastry

½ batch No-Fail Shortcrust Pastry, page 130, rolled to fit a 10-inch (24-cm) quiche dish, chilled in the refrigerator until needed

Filling

2 cups (475 mL) thinly sliced zucchini (use a mandoline—see page 29—or a sharp knife)
1 bunch green onions, chopped
2 large red peppers, roasted, peeled and diced (see page 82)
5 oz (140 gr) feta cheese (sheep, cow or goat), crumbled

Custard

5 large or 6 medium eggs
1 cup (250 mL) light cream
2 Tbsp (30 mL) unbleached white flour
½ tsp (2.5 mL) salt
½ tsp (2.5 mL) fresh-ground pepper

Garnish (optional)

¼ cup (60 mL) Garlic Scape Pesto (see page 150)

Preheat oven to 400F (205C).

Fill crust with layers of the vegetables. Cover with the feta cheese. In a food blender, blend the custard ingredients until smooth, and pour over the filling in the dish.

If desired, place teaspoon-sized dollops of Garlic Scape Pesto on top of the custard before the quiche goes into the oven.

Reduce the oven to 350F (175C) and bake on the middle shelf for 25 minutes. To prevent excess browning, cover the dish with foil and bake for another 20 to 30 minutes, until the centre has set and is firm to the touch. Leave to cool for 10 minutes before serving.

Makes 6 to 8 servings

Zucchini Ribbons with Rice VG* GF

This recipe is tasty served alone or as an accompaniment to other dishes. To prepare, you will need a spiralizer slicer (see page 29).

- 2 garlic cloves, minced
- 1 Tbsp (15 mL) butter or vegetable oil
- 2 cups (475 mL) zucchini ribbons
- 3 medium tomatoes, chopped
- ½ cup (125 mL) peas, fresh or frozen, shelled
- 1 Tbsp (15 mL) Fines Herbes Salées du Bas-du-Fleuve (see page 58)
- 1 Tbsp (15 mL) Bragg Liquid Aminos
- 2 tsp (10 mL) fresh-ground pepper
- 2 cups (475 mL) long-grain brown rice, cooked
- Parmigiano-Reggiano cheese, grated to taste

Sauté the garlic in the butter or oil until soft.

Add the zucchini ribbons with other vegetables and seasonings and simmer for about 10 minutes over low heat, until the veggies are juicy.

* if you use oil and omit the butter and garnish

Blend in the cooked long-grain brown rice.

Optional: Serve sprinkled with grated Parmigiano-Reggiano.

Makes 4 to 6 servings

Amber's Vegan Veggie Burgers

Patties can be stored in a freezer container, between layers of waxed paper. You can also roll this recipe into balls for a hot appetizer served with a cocktail stick, or use them as "meatballs" in Garden Tomato Sauce (see page 205). Delicious with Aioli Sauce (next page).

2 Tbsp (30 mL) vegetable oil, plus extra for sautéing the patties

1 small onion, chopped

1 garlic clove, minced

½ cup (125 mL) diced mushrooms

½ cup (125 mL) almonds

½ cup (125 mL) sunflower seeds

1 cup (250 mL) cooked pinto, Romano or black beans

½ cup (125 mL) parsley and/or cilantro, minced

1 cup (250 mL) cooked quinoa (see Perfect Quinoa, page 35)

1 cup (250 mL) oat flakes

1 cup (250 mL) carrots, grated

¼ cup (60 mL) tamari soy sauce

¼ cup (60 mL) Bragg Liquid Aminos

½ cup (125 mL) whole wheat flour

½ Tbsp (7 mL) cumin, ground or seeds

½ Tbsp (7 mL) chili powder

½ Tbsp (7 mL) dried oregano

Heat the oil and sauté the onion and garlic together for 5 minutes. Add the mushrooms and sauté all together for another 10 minutes, or until soft. Remove from the heat.

Meanwhile, roast the almonds and sunflower seeds by spreading them on a baking sheet and baking at 350F (175C) for 5 minutes on 1 side, then turning and roasting for another 5 minutes or so until light brown and fragrant. Allow to cool, then coarsely chop the nuts in a food processor or with a sharp knife.

Mix the rest of the ingredients into the food processor and blend well.

Scoop up enough of the mixture to roll into a round the size of a golf ball or shape into larger balls and press them between the palms of your hands to form into hamburger bun-sized patties. If too wet, add more flour until the mixture sticks well.

Sauté the balls or patties in vegetable oil over medium heat for 10 minutes on each side, or brush lightly with oil and grill them on the barbecue.

Makes 8 patties or 20 "meatballs"

Aioli Sauce GF

This fantastic "garlic mayonnaise" is worth whisking for! It enhances the flavour of burgers, wraps, paninis, sandwiches, calzones and pizza, and is also great with fish dishes—a classic for wild salmon.

4 garlic cloves, peeled but not chopped
½ tsp (2.5 mL) coarse or sea salt
1 large egg yolk
½ tsp (2.5 mL) Dijon mustard
¼ cup (60 mL) extra virgin olive oil
3 Tbsp (45 mL) vegetable oil
½ lemon, zest and juice
Salt and pepper to taste

Using the blade of a heavy knife, or a pestle and mortar, mash the garlic cloves and salt to a paste-like consistency.

Whisk the egg yolk and the mustard together. Combine the oils. Drizzle the oil slowly into the yolk mixture, whisking constantly, until the oil is gone and the mixture has emulsified. TIP: If the aioli is too thick, whisk in a few drops of water.

Whisk in the garlic paste and the lemon zest and juice. Adjust seasoning if needed with salt and pepper. Cover and chill until ready to use and keep refrigerated for up to three days.

Optional: Add basil or dill for a nice variation.

Makes ½ cup (125 mL)

When garlic bulbs come out of the ground, they need to be hung to dry for several weeks to cure them for storage. Once cured, softneck varieties can be braided to make attractive garlic ropes for hanging in the kitchen. If stored in containers, they should have ventilation to prevent the garlic bulbs from rotting.

Ratatouille Casserole GF

This dish tastes great hot or cold, served alone and especially on top of a heap of broad egg noodles.

- 1 large eggplant, cubed
- **1 Tbsp (15 mL) coarse salt**
- 1 large zucchini, cubed
- 1 medium onion, diced
- 1 red pepper, seeded and diced
- 4 oz (112 gr) mushrooms, diced
- 2 garlic cloves, minced
- 1½ cups (350 mL) Garden Tomato Sauce (see page 205)
- 6 large fresh tomatoes, chopped
- 20 leaves fresh basil, thinly sliced or 2 tsp (10 mL) dried basil
- **1 Tbsp (15 mL) Bragg Liquid Aminos**
- **1 tsp (5 mL) sea salt**
- **1 tsp (5 mL) fresh-ground pepper**
- **Parmigiano-Reggiano cheese, grated for garnish (optional)**

Toss the eggplant with the salt. Leave to sweat and lose bitterness for 2 to 3 hours.

Preheat oven to 375F (190C).

Rinse and drain. Toss all the ingredients in a large bowl. Place the mixture in a large casserole dish and put the lid on or cover with foil. Reduce the oven to 350F (175C) and bake the casserole for 45 minutes. Adjust seasonings to taste.

If desired, sprinkle with freshly grated Parmigiano-Reggiano as you serve it up.

Makes 4 servings

'Rosa bianca' eggplant (Solanum melongena) is an Italian heirloom with large, creamy-white and lavender-pink fruits. It's a heat lover well suited to container growing as well as in the garden, ready for harvest 70 to 85 days from transplant depending on the summer!

Cauliflower Curry Wrap

Use wraps of your choice: whole wheat, multigrain, sundried tomato or gluten-free. We often use leftovers as filling for wraps for a tasty meal in a snap! For a variation on this recipe, try quinoa instead of rice.

1 cup (250 mL) basmati rice, washed

2 cups (475 mL) cold water

1 bay leaf (optional)

3 Tbsp (45 mL) extra virgin olive oil

1 large onion, finely chopped

3 garlic cloves, minced

2 tsp (10 mL) garam masala (see page 241) or curry powder

1 large red pepper, diced

1½ cups (350 mL) garbanzo beans (chickpeas), cooked

1 medium cauliflower, cut into quarters, leaves and core removed, broken into small florets

1 cup (250 mL) Garden Tomato Sauce (see page 205)

6 large wrap shells of your choice

Put the rice and water into a saucepan with a tight-fitting lid. Bring to the boil with the lid off, and then reduce the heat to low. Cook for 15 minutes for white rice, or 30 minutes for brown rice, with the lid on. No peeking and the rice will be light and fluffy! TIP: Add a bay leaf to impart a delicate flavour to the rice.

Sauté the onion and garlic in the oil for 5 minutes until softened. Stir in the garam masala or curry powder to warm the spices. Add the pepper, beans, cauliflower florets and tomato sauce. Reduce the heat. Sauté gently for 10 minutes or until the vegetables are tender. Stir in the cooked rice.

Lay out the wrap and spread the curried cauliflower/rice mixture over it to ½-inch (1-cm) thickness, leaving the edges free of filling. Fold both sides of the wrap into the centre and holding them in, roll up tightly from one end to the other. Place on a baking sheet so that the seam side is on the bottom. Bake in the oven for 10 to 15 minutes at 350F (175C) so that the wrap is lightly toasted.

Cut in half and serve with the chutney of your choice.

Makes 6 large wraps

Fava Bean Couscous

My husband, Guy, goes nuts for fresh favas (broad beans) from the summer garden. Fava beans are delicious when steamed and served with olive oil, lemon and salt. They also make a wonderful addition to pasta and grains, as in this tasty recipe. Freeze fresh (unshelled) beans on a baking sheet, then transfer to a freezer bag or container so that you can enjoy succulent buttery beans anytime.

1½ lb (700 gr) fresh fava bean pods

1¼ cup (300 mL) water

1 cup (250 mL) Israeli couscous*

¼ cup (60 mL) extra virgin olive oil

1 large shallot, finely chopped

1 tsp (5 mL) salt

1 tsp (5 mL) fresh-ground black pepper

1 lemon, zest and juice

2 Tbsp (30 mL) fresh mint leaves, thinly sliced

To extract the beans from their skins,** bring a medium pot of water to the boil and boil the beans for 2 minutes, until the skins have loosened. Using a slotted spoon, transfer the beans into an ice water bath, reserving the cooking water in the pot. Pierce each fava and squeeze the inner green bean out, discarding the skin into the compost. Set aside.

Add the couscous to the pot. Bring the bean water back to the boil. Turn off the heat, add a lid and leave the couscous to soak for 15 minutes. (Drain off extra liquid if necessary.)

Heat the olive oil in a skillet, and sauté the shallot with the salt and black pepper, stirring frequently until golden brown, about 5 minutes. Reduce the heat, add the prepared fava beans and sauté until they are tender, about a minute (longer if the beans are still in their skins, or frozen). Add the couscous and lemon juice. Adjust seasoning if necessary.

Serve garnished with the mint and zest.

Makes 4 servings as a main course, 6 as a side dish

* Israeli couscous is a pearl shaped, lightly toasted pasta. If it isn't available, try substituting orzo pasta—just cook according to package directions.

** This recipe includes a step to skin the beans, as the slightly chewy skins detract from the buttery nature of the inner bean. However, when in a hurry for dinner, we are happy to eat fresh beans skin and all!

Mediterranean Stuffed Grape Leaves

This is food at its most rustic and sensual. The bite-sized stuffed leaves (or dolmades) are great as an appetizer or side dish. The taste is sweet and tangy from the combination of currants or raisins, mint and vinegar.

About 40 palm-sized grape leaves, or 80 smaller leaves*

Filling

1 cup (250 mL) rice, cooked

¼ **cup (60 mL) green onions, minced**

½ **cup (125 mL) celery, chopped**

½ **cup (125 mL) fresh mint leaves, finely chopped**

2 Tbsp (30 mL) extra virgin olive oil

2 tsp (10 mL) white wine vinegar

2 tsp (10 mL) lemon juice

⅓ **cup (80 mL) currants or golden raisins**

¼ **cup (60 mL) sunflower seeds**

1 tsp (5 mL) sea salt

½ **tsp (2.5 mL) black pepper**

1 Tbsp (15 mL) nasturtium capers (see page 156)

Rinse the leaves in a bowl of cold water, and drain. Divide leaves into tidy stacks of 20 each, roll them up like a fat cigar and tie them together with string. Drop the "cigar" into a pot of boiling salted water, remove straight away and plunge into a pot of cold water. Now they are ready to use. TIP: At this stage, the leaf rolls can also be frozen in plastic freezer bags for later use.

Preheat oven to 350F (175C).

In a large bowl, combine all the filling ingredients above and toss well.

Put 1½ Tbsp (22 mL) of the filling on the leaf (or leaves), fold the outer edges of the leaf in and roll up tightly. Repeat.

Arrange the filled grape leaves in a glass or ceramic baking dish and drizzle with a little olive oil and lemon juice, ensuring that each leaf gets coated.

Pour ¼ inch (5 mm) of water into the baking dish. Cover with a lid (or foil), and bake for 30 to 45 minutes, until the leaves are tender.

Serve warm or cold.

Makes about 40 dolmades

* For tender dolmades, it is best to choose slightly smaller, less-mature leaves (closest to the end of the vine), but big enough to roll around the filling—the size of the palm of your hand is ideal. If your grape leaves are very small, use two per dolmades by placing grape leaves stem-end to stem-end with a slight overlap (as shown in the photo). If you don't have grapevines in the garden, grape leaves preserved in brine can be purchased in most supermarkets. Rinse the brine off by separating the leaves in a bowl of cold water and omit the salt from the filling.

Planked Wild Salmon

This much-loved dish, courtesy Bruce Wood of Bruce's Kitchen on Salt Spring Island, is the perfect way to enjoy my catch of the day—the cedar plank perfumes the dish with a sweet smokiness. When you buy cedar for the plank, ensure it is untreated. Most fish stores sell these planks.

Marinate the salmon ahead of time—at least 1 hour and up to 2 days—for the best flavour.

4 Tbsp (60 mL) fresh dill, chopped

1 tsp (5 mL) mustard seeds, cracked

¼ cup (60 mL) brown sugar

½ tsp (2.5 mL) coarsely ground black pepper

2 tsp (10 mL) coarse sea salt

4 × 6 oz (170 gr) boneless wild salmon fillets

1 lemon, cut in half

2 oz (56 gr) brandy or dark rum

1 cedar plank (½ inch thick × 6 inches wide x 12 inches long/1 × 15 × 30 cm), soaked in water for 1 hour before grilling

In a bowl, mix together the dill, mustard seeds, brown sugar, black pepper and salt.

Place the salmon fillets in a non-reactive dish and rub with the lemon halves. Rub the salmon fillets with the dill mixture and drizzle with the brandy or rum. Cover and refrigerate a minimum of 1 hour or as long as 48 hours.

Preheat the barbecue to medium-high.

Put the salmon on the plank and place the plank on the barbecue. Close the lid and cook until the salmon is opaque and flakes, approximately 12 to 14 minutes. Serve hot with Garlic Scape Pesto (page 150) or Ailoli Sauce (page 164).

Makes 4 servings

SUMMER DESSERTS

Jolene's Peach Pies

It wouldn't be summer without a fresh fruit pie—whether strawberry-rhubarb, apple-blackberry or the divine peach recipe included here. Once you have mastered No-Fail Shortcrust Pastry, you'll be able to whip together pies in no time. This recipe makes two pies—one for eating now and one for the freezer. I guarantee that when you eat this peach pie in winter it will knock your socks off!

Double batch No-Fail Shortcrust Pastry (see page 130)

4 lbs (1.8 kg) tree-ripened peaches, blanched to remove skins and sliced into eighths

1½ cups (350 mL) berry or granulated sugar

⅓ cup (80 mL) quick tapioca (or tapioca flour) whisked with ½ cup (125 mL) berry or granulated sugar

1½ tsp (7.5 mL) cinnamon

2 Tbsp (30 mL) butter

1 Tbsp (15 mL) cream

Cinnamon sugar (1 Tbsp (15 mL) sugar mixed with 1 tsp (5 mL) cinnamon)

Whipping cream (optional)

Preheat oven 375F.

Put the sliced peaches in a large saucepan with 1½ cups (350 mL) of the sugar and stir to mix. Let stand for 5 minutes. Bring to a boil and cook for 1 minute stirring constantly. Add the tapioca starch mixture and cinnamon, and continue to cook and stir for 1 minute.

Roll the pastry into 4 circles large enough to drap over pie dishes. Line the pie dishes with pastry. Pour half the peach filling over it to fill each pie dish, and dot the filling with butter. Place the pastry 'lids' over the filling; fold the two edges of the pastry underneath to create a smooth edge; crimp the pastry between your fingers to create a decorative edge and seal the pie filling.

For a shiny golden-brown fruit pie, brush a thin layer of cream over the pastry and sprinkle it all over with cinnamon sugar. Prick 3 slits into the pastry with a knife to release steam while baking.

Reduce oven heat to 350F (175C) and bake for 30 to 35 minutes. Allow to stand until juices thicken and then serve hot or cold with a dollop of whipped cream.

Makes two 8-inch (20-cm) covered pies

To freeze a baked fruit pie, allow it to cool in the pie dish. Wrap the pie, dish and all, in plastic wrap and then slide inside a large labelled freezer bag. The day you are ready to enjoy your second pie, remove the pie from the freezer in the morning, take it out of the bag and allow it time to thaw. Remove plastic wrap and warm in a preheated oven at 350F (175C) for 25 to 30 minutes. Fruit pies in winter bring the taste of summer back to the table.

Rhubarb Strawberry Galettes

I guarantee these appealing fruity delights will not last long, as they look so good and are delicious!

Pastry

   2 cups (475 mL) unbleached white flour (or use half white and half whole wheat flour)
   ½ tsp (2.5 mL) salt
   ½ tsp (2.5 mL) five-spice powder (equal parts cinnamon powder, allspice, ground cloves, mace, grated nutmeg)
   ¾ cup (180 mL) unsalted butter, cut into pieces
   ¼ cup (60 mL) cold water
   2 Tbsp (30 mL) lemon juice

Filling

   2 cups (475 mL) fresh rhubarb, chopped into 1-inch (2.5-cm) pieces
   ½ lb (225 gr) fresh strawberries, quartered
   ²/₃ cup (160 mL) granulated sugar
   3 Tbsp (45 mL) unbleached white flour
   1 tsp (5 mL) five-spice powder (cinnamon powder, allspice, ground cloves, mace, grated nutmeg)

Glaze

   1 egg yolk
   1 Tbsp (15 mL) milk or cream

Pastry

Preheat oven to 425F (220C).

Combine the flour, salt and five-spice powder. Cut in the butter until the mixture resembles small peas. Combine the cold water and lemon juice and sprinkle over the flour mixture. Using your hands, bring the pastry together into a ball, adding extra water if necessary. Wrap in a damp tea towel and chill in the refrigerator for 30 minutes.

Filling

In a large bowl, toss all the above ingredients together.

Pastry

Cut the chilled pastry into 6 equal pieces. Roll each piece into a 6-inch (15-mL) circle and transfer the rounds to a parchment-lined baking sheet. Divide the filling between each round, leaving a 2-inch (5-mL) edge clear all the way around. Fold the edge of the pastry over the filling to enclose, leaving the centre open, like a partially-closed drawstring bag.

Glaze

Beat together the egg yolk and the milk or cream. Brush the glaze over the pastry with a pastry brush. Optional: Sprinkle with a little sugar.

Bake the galettes for 15 minutes at 450F (230C), and then reduce the heat to 350F (175C). Bake for another 20 minutes until the pastry is golden in colour. Remove from the oven and leave to cool before serving.

Makes 6 servings

Fruity Carrot Cupcakes

These carrot cupcakes are so moist and delectable, especially with the frosting on top, that it's hard to eat only one!

1 cup (250 mL) unbleached flour

1 tsp (5 mL) baking soda

1 tsp (5 mL) baking powder

¼ tsp (1 mL) sea salt

1 tsp (5 mL) cinnamon powder

¼ tsp (1 mL) fresh-grated nutmeg

¾ cup (180 mL) raw cane sugar

½ cup (125 mL) vegetable oil—coconut or grapeseed

2 large eggs

½ tsp (2.5 mL) pure vanilla extract

1½ cup (350 mL) carrots, grated

8 oz (225 gr) pineapple (canned or fresh), chopped

½ cup (125 mL) currants

1/3 cup (80 mL) walnuts, chopped

1 batch Cream Cheese Frosting (page 143)

Berries and/or walnuts for garnish

Preheat oven to 350F (175C).

Line a muffin pan with 10 large-sized paper baking cups or parchment paper squares.

Sift the flour, baking soda, baking powder, salt, cinnamon and nutmeg together through a fine-mesh sieve. Stir well.

Whisk the sugar, oil, eggs and vanilla to combine thoroughly. Using a wooden spoon, mix the wet and the dry ingredients together to form a batter.

Mix the carrots, pineapple, currants and walnuts together and stir into the batter. Spoon the batter into the baking cups to two-thirds full.

Bake for 25 minutes, or until the cupcakes are firm to the touch in the centre.

When the cupcakes have cooled, pipe or spread on the frosting and decorate each cupcake with finely chopped walnuts and/or a berry on top. Refrigerate to set icing.

Makes 12 cupcakes

Strawberry Lemon Scones with Devonshire Cream

I first met my husband, Guy, over a plate of these scones. We're still together after many years of happily eating scones, so I had to include this recipe! Start the Devonshire cream a day ahead.

Devonshire Cream

½ cup (125 mL) sour cream

½ cup (125 mL) whipping cream

Mix equal parts sour cream and whipping cream in an open glass jar and leave overnight in the fridge. That's it!

Scones

2 cups (475 mL) unbleached white flour, unsifted

2 Tbsp (30 mL) granulated sugar

1 Tbsp (15 mL) baking powder

¼ tsp (1 mL) sea salt

4 Tbsp (60 mL) cold unsalted butter, cut into small pieces

2 eggs

½ cup (125 mL) heavy cream plus 2 Tbsp (30 mL) for egg wash

Zest of 2 lemons

1 egg yolk

Preheat oven to 400F (205C).

Sift flour, sugar, baking powder and salt into a bowl. Cut in the chilled pieces of butter, using 2 knives or a pastry blender, until the mixture resembles coarse bread crumbs.

Whisk the eggs with ½ cup (125 mL) heavy cream and add the lemon zest. Stir into the flour mixture using a fork, until a sticky dough forms. Turn the dough out onto a lightly floured board and bring it together with your hands until it forms a smooth ball. TIP: Handle the dough as little as possible for best results.

Using a rolling pin, lightly roll (or pat the dough with your hands) into a large round of even

1-inch (2.5-cm) thickness. Using a glass (dip the rim in flour first to prevent sticking) or a round cookie cutter, make 6 rounds. Place the rounds 1 inch (2.5 cm) apart on a greased or parchment-lined baking sheet.

Whisk 2 Tbsp (30 mL) cream together with the egg yolk, and brush the top of the scone rounds with this egg wash.

Reduce the oven to 350F (175C) and bake about 15 to 20 minutes, until the scones are golden brown on top and have risen to light and fluffy.

Cool on wire racks.

Continued on next page

Filling

- **2 cups (475 mL) strawberries, hulled and halved**
- **1 lemon, juiced**
- **¼ cup (60 mL) granulated sugar**

Chop the strawberries and mix with the lemon juice and sugar.

Leave to stand about 1 hour, until the berries have released their juice.

Slice the scones in half and add a dollop of Devonshire cream onto each half. Top with a spoonful of strawberries and serve open-faced.

Makes 6 servings

Fragaria vesca *(woodland strawberries) make a wonderful groundcover and can also be grown in a half oak barrel, as in this photo. The plants produce small, sweet and irresistible berries from June to November. The best part is that these strawberries are easy and fast to grow from seed.*

Berry Yummy Sponge Cake

This Norwegian recipe from my friend Mildred is a delightful way to use all those berries in the garden. Choose from tayberry, blueberry, raspberry, strawberry, blackberry or gooseberry. It's fast to make and wonderful to eat. Serve this with a cuppa, and say, "Yes, I grew them myself!"

1 cup (250 mL) raw cane sugar

¾ cup (180 mL) butter

2 large eggs

Zest of 1 lemon

2 Tbsp (30 mL) milk

1 tsp (5 mL) pure vanilla extract

¾ cup (180 mL) unbleached white flour

¾ cup (180 mL) whole wheat flour

1½ tsp (7 mL) baking powder

Pinch salt (if using unsalted butter)

2 cups (475 mL) fresh or frozen berries of your choice

Preheat oven to 350F (175C).

Lightly grease a 9 × 13-inch (23 × 33-cm) baking pan.

Beat the sugar and the butter until smooth and creamy. Whisk together the eggs, lemon zest, milk and vanilla extract.

Sift the dry ingredients together. Using a wooden spoon, gradually blend dry ingredients into the wet ingredients to form a stiff but smooth batter. Using a spatula, spread this batter evenly into the baking pan.

Press the fresh berries generously into the batter to cover the whole area. You can use berries from the freezer for year-round sponges.

Reduce the oven to 325F (160C) and bake for 30 minutes, or until the sponge is lightly browned on top and feels firm to the touch. Test with a toothpick to make sure the sponge is cooked in the centre.

Leave to cool and cut into squares for serving.

Makes 12 servings

Fresh Fruit Pops `VG*` `GF`

Try these for a nourishing alternative to store-bought Popsicles dosed with artificial ingredients. There's no end to the fruity combinations you can prepare. When parched kids come home, it's great to have these cooling treats handy in the freezer.

> **2 cups (475 mL) fresh apple juice**
> **2 cups (475 mL) berries fresh or frozen**
> **1 large ripe banana**

Or try this instead:

> **1 cup (250 mL) plain yogourt**
> **1 cup (250 mL) berries, fresh or frozen**
> **1 large ripe banana**
> **¾ cup (180 mL) apple juice**
> **1 Tbsp (15 mL) honey or maple syrup (if you prefer it sweeter)**

Blend in a food processor to reach a smooth consistency. TIP: If too thick, add more juice and blend again.

Pour into moulds and place the sticks into the liquid before freezing.

Makes 4 pops

* if you use soy yogourt and maple syrup

These tayberries are large and juicy and make wonderful pies and desserts. Fast to establish, productive trailing canes work well twining over arbours or pergolas. For the sweetest flavour, plant berries in full sun; for the best production, feed the soil around the roots every year with good-quality compost mulch.

SUMMER DRINKS

Blueberry Iced Tea VG GF

This wonderful fruity twist to iced tea is always appreciated on a hot summer day!

5 teabags or 5 tsp (25 mL) loose rooibos tea

8 cups (2 L) boiling water

2½ cups (600 mL) fresh blueberries

1 cup (250 mL) water

¼ cup (60 mL) maple syrup

1 Tbsp (15 mL) lemon juice

Lemon wedges

Ice cubes

Make tea by steeping the rooibos teabags (or loose tea in a tea ball) in boiling water for 10 minutes. Remove the teabags or the tea ball.

In a large pot, bring the blueberries and 1 cup (250 mL) water to the boil. Reduce the heat and simmer for 5 minutes while stirring. Add the maple syrup and tea to the berries. Turn off the heat and leave to cool.

Strain the mixture through a cheesecloth-lined sieve into a pitcher or jug, so that the tea liquid stays clear. Stir in the lemon juice. Refrigerate for about 2 hours until cold.

Serve over ice with lemon wedges.

Makes 4 to 6 servings

Raspberry Lemon Verbena Iced Tea VG GF

Lemon verbena is a deciduous shrub infused with an intense lemon flavour (and for more on this lovely herb, see page 59). I love the combination of raspberries and lemon in this version of iced tea.

5 teabags or 5 tsp (25 mL) loose rooibos tea

1 good sprig of fresh lemon verbena leaves

8 cups (2 L) boiling water

2½ cups (600 mL) fresh raspberries

1 cup (250 mL) water

¼ cup (60 mL) maple syrup

Lemon wedges

Ice cubes

Make tea by steeping the rooibos teabags (or loose tea in a tea ball) and the lemon verbena leaves stripped off the stems in the boiling water for 10 minutes. Remove the teabags or the tea ball. Scoop out the lemon verbena leaves.

Bring the raspberries and 1 cup (250 mL) of water to the boil. Reduce the heat and simmer for 5 minutes while stirring. Add the maple syrup and the tea. Leave to cool.

Strain through a cheesecloth-lined sieve into a pitcher or jug, so that the beverage stays clear. Refrigerate about 2 hours until cold.

Serve over ice with lemon wedges.

Makes 4 to 6 servings

Mrs. Marsh's Raspberry Cordial VG GF

This refreshing summer drink always surprises and delights. Serve over ice, with a good splash of club soda or sparkling mineral water.

5 lb (2.3 kg) fresh raspberries
½ cup (125 mL) white wine vinegar
½ cup (125 mL) water
Granulated sugar

In a saucepan, mash the berries (I use a potato masher for this). Mix the water and the vinegar and pour over fruit until covered. Cover the pan with a lid and leave to sit for 48 hours.

Mash again. Strain through a cheesecloth-lined sieve into a saucepan. For each 1 cup (250 mL) of juice, add 1 cup (250 mL) of sugar. Slowly bring to the boil, stirring to dissolve the sugar. Pour the hot juice into a sterilized glass bottle or jar. TIP: Leave the bottle or jar filled with hot water before filling so it doesn't crack.

Makes 3 cups (700 mL)

RASPBERRY COCKTAIL

Turn this cordial into a wonderful cocktail by blending it with an equal amount of cherry liqueur (see next page) and adding a splash of club soda or sparkling mineral water to taste.

Fresh Fruit Liqueurs VG GF

This is a great way to enjoy homegrown berries and fruits, and just a few sips will make you feel like celebrating! Mix bitter berries such as cranberries and currants with sweeter choices such as blueberries and strawberries to make a successful mixed-berry liqueur. Fruits, such as cherries, should be macerated lightly in a food processor, and berries should be lightly mashed to release some liquid.

1 lb (454 gr) berries or fruit
**3 cups (700 mL) 80-proof vodka (the alcohol content should be around 30% for fruit
    liqueurs)**
Granulated sugar

Wash the fruit or berries. Fill a sterilized 1-quart (1-L) Mason jar with the fruit or berries. Top up the jar with vodka to cover the fruit. Place the lid and ring on the jar and store in a cool, dark place, shaking once a week for 4 weeks.

After 4 weeks, strain the fruit through a cheesecloth-lined sieve, until all the liquid passes through. Using a measuring cup, transfer the clear liquid back into the cleaned jar, and add 1¼ cup (300 mL) granulated sugar for every cup of liquid. Put the lid on tightly and give the jar a good shake to dissolve the sugar. Store in a cool, dark cupboard.

TIP: To make a 40-proof dessert, use the fruit from the cheesecloth to make a fool (not of yourself!). Simply mix the fruit with an equal volume of whipped cream and leave in the fridge to cool.

For maximum taste, fruit and berry liqueurs should be stored at least 6 months, because the flavour improves during storage. (However, for special occasions you can peek in at 3 months.) Pour the clear fruit liqueur into a presentation bottle (fun to shop for in a thrift shop) and be proud to say "Yes, I made it myself!"

FALL

FALL RECIPES

Baked potatoes.

FALL STARTERS

Roasted Pumpkin Seeds VG GF

It's a shame to waste the nutritious seeds when you scoop pumpkins out in fall. They are packed with fibre, vitamins, minerals and numerous health-promoting antioxidants. Here's a simple way to enjoy them as a snack or added to salads and grain recipes.

Seeds of 1 large pumpkin—about 2 cups (475 mL)
3 Tbsp (45 mL) vegetable oil
1 tsp (5 mL) sea salt

Preheat oven to 375F (190C).

Scoop the seeds out of the pumpkin. Put them into a large bowl and fill the bowl with water. Swish the seeds around, so that good seeds float and the stringy bits separate off. Drain and dry well, so that they will roast faster.

In a large bowl, toss the seeds with the oil. Sprinkle lightly with the sea salt. Spread the seeds onto a baking sheet in a single layer, and roast for 15 to 20 minutes in the preheated oven, until they are crispy golden brown. Leave to cool.

Store in an airtight glass jar.

TIP: For crispier seeds, place the cleaned pumpkin seeds in a small saucepan, half full of water and add 1 tsp (5 mL) salt. Cover and simmer gently until softened, for about 2 hours. Drain and spread onto a baking sheet and leave until dry. Coat with the oil and bake as above, without adding more salt.

Makes 2 cups (475 mL)

Growing a selection of winter squash insures you'll have plenty for delicious soups, casseroles and roasting throughout winter. They thrive best when grown in fertile soil in full sun. Choose good storage varieties such as hubbard, sweet dumpling, butternut, banana, acorn and pumpkin.

Cheesy Corn Bread

This is simply s'more-ish by itself and also with soups, salads and casseroles. Tuck some into the kids' lunchboxes for a treat. Like most quick breads, this is best eaten within a day.

¼ **cup (60 mL) extra virgin olive oil**

½ **cup (125 mL) green onions, chopped**

1 **cup (250 mL) unbleached or whole wheat flour**

1 **cup (250 mL) yellow corn meal**

2 **Tbsp (30 mL) baking powder**

1 **tsp (5 mL) sea salt**

1 **large egg**

1 **Tbsp (15 mL) liquid honey**

1 **cup (250 mL) milk**

1 **cup (250 mL) corn kernels, fresh or frozen**

½ **cup (125 mL) aged white cheddar cheese**

Preheat oven to 375F (190C).

Sauté the green onions in the oil until translucent. Set aside to cool.

In a large bowl, mix together the dry ingredients.

In a medium bowl, beat the egg with the honey and milk.

Add the wet to the dry ingredients and blend to a smooth batter consistency.

Add the sautéed onions (with all the oil) and the corn kernels and cheese to the batter.

Blend together with a wooden spoon and spread the batter into a greased 8-inch (20-cm) square baking pan.

Reduce oven heat to 350F (175C) and bake for 30 to 35 minutes, until the top is firm and lightly browned, and a toothpick inserted in the centre comes out clean.

Makes sixteen 2-inch (5-cm) square servings

Creamy Chanterelle Mushroom Soup VG* GF

We always look forward to wild mushroom season.

¼ cup (60 mL) butter or vegetable oil

1 large onion, chopped

3 garlic cloves, minced

2 dried bay leaves

1 lb (454 gr) chanterelle or seasonal mushrooms, chopped into ½-inch (1-cm) cubes

2 cups (475 mL) veggie stock or water

½ tsp (2.5 mL) fresh-ground black pepper

1 Tbsp (15 mL) Worcestershire sauce

1 Tbsp (15 mL) Fines Herbes Salées du Bas-du-Fleuve (see page 58) or choose herbs from chervil, parsley, tarragon, dill, sweet marjoram or oregano

2 cups (475 mL) milk, soy milk or cream

2 Tbsp (30 mL) cornstarch

¼ cup (60 mL) milk

Salt to taste

Heat the butter or oil and sauté the onions with the garlic and bay leaves for 5 minutes. Add the mushrooms and sauté for another 5 minutes over medium heat. Cover the mushrooms with the veggie stock or water and season with the black pepper, Worcestershire sauce and herbs. Allow to heat, but not to boil. Simmer gently for 15 minutes over medium heat.

Slowly whisk in the milk (or cream to make a richer soup). Make a paste with the cornstarch and the milk. Stir the paste into the soup with a wooden spoon to thicken. Remove the bay leaf before serving.

Makes 6 to 8 servings

* if you use soy milk

This is what three pounds of freshly harvested chanterelles look like. I dried half of them and used the rest fresh for this soup and a pasta dish. What a treat!

West Coast Wild Salmon Chowder `GF*`

Last summer I put up a "Gone Fishing!" sign and spent the day on my friend Ann's boat doing just that. The result was five salmon, plenty to barbecue, smoke and prepare this delicious rich soup. I was so proud to say "Yes, I caught it myself!"

3 Tbsp (45 mL) extra virgin olive oil

1 large onion, diced

3 garlic cloves, minced

2 bay leaves

4 carrots, diced

6 large potatoes, diced

1 red pepper, diced

½ cup (125 mL) peas, fresh shelled or frozen

8 cups (2 L) fish stock (made from heads and spines of fish)

1 lemon, peel and zest

½ tsp (2.5 mL) nutmeg, grated

1 Tbsp (15 mL) fresh dill or 1 tsp (5 mL) dried

1½ tsp (7 mL) sea salt

1 tsp (5 mL) fresh-ground black pepper

Dash of Tabasco sauce

Dash of Worcestershire sauce

2 cups (475 mL) wild salmon chunks

2 cups (475 mL) light cream, milk or soy milk

2 Tbsp (30 mL) unbleached white flour or cornstarch

3 Tbsp (45 mL) milk or soy milk

1 Tbsp (15 mL) parsley, finely minced

Heat the oil, and sauté the onion, garlic and bay leaves until softened, for about 5 minutes. Add the rest of the vegetables and sauté over medium heat for another 10 minutes, until the vegetables have softened.

Cover with the fish stock, add the seasonings including lemon zest and bring to the boil. Reduce the heat. Add chunks of salmon and the light cream, milk or soy milk, depending on how creamy you want your soup to be.

Thicken the soup by stirring the flour or cornstarch into 3 Tbsp (45 mL) milk to make a smooth paste. Blend the paste into the soup and bring back to hot, but do not allow to boil. Simmer gently for 20 minutes to allow flavours to meld.

Serve garnished with finely minced parsley.

Makes 10 servings

* if you use cornstarch for thickening

Sabine's Italian Minestrone

Cavolo nero or 'Lacinato' kale is an essential ingredient of Italian minestrone, at least Sabine's version. She says the trick is to add the vegetables one after the other rather than all together. Minestrone tastes even better a day or two later, because the flavour develops with time.

¼ cup (60 mL) extra virgin olive oil

1 large onion, red or white, chopped

2 carrots, chopped

2 celery stalks

1 leek

2 potatoes

1 good bunch of Cavolo nero or 'Lacinato' kale, shredded (mid-ribs removed if tough)

½ medium-sized Savoy cabbage

6 cups (1.5 L) vegetable broth

1½ cups (350 mL) cannelloni beans, cooked

10 large fresh tomatoes, chopped (or 28-oz/796-mL can of tomatoes)

2 Tbsp fresh herbs—sage, thyme, summer savory, oregano, parsley or basil (optional)

Salt and pepper to taste

Freshly grated Parmigiano-Reggiano cheese

Pour the olive oil over the base of a large saucepan. Stir in the onion and sauté for 5 minutes over medium-high heat. Add the carrots and stir, and then chop and stir your way through the celery, leek, potatoes and kale. If the mixture looks dry, add a little broth to help the mass to slowly reduce. Chop the cabbage, and throw it into the pot with enough broth to cover the vegetables. Let everything simmer for 15 minutes.

Add the beans and tomatoes and fresh herbs if desired. Leave the soup to simmer over low heat for an hour, stirring every now and then to prevent the bottom from sticking. Season with salt and pepper to taste and serve with some freshly grated Parmigiano-Reggiano on top.

Buon appetito!

Makes 10 to 12 servings

* if you leave out the Parmigiano-Reggiano cheese

Kale is a fast-growing annual that provides bundles of nutritious greens all year from a spring or a fall sowing. 'Lacinato' kale, with its coarse texture and strong flavour, is ideally suited to making warming soups.

Beans with Minty Yogourt Sauce

I love eating fresh-picked green beans, but serving them this way elevates the experience to a delicious new level.

- **1 lb (454 gr) green beans, topped and tailed**
- **¼ cup (60 mL) almond or extra virgin olive oil**
- **2 garlic cloves, minced**
- **1 Tbsp (15 mL) white wine vinegar**
- **4 green onions, finely chopped**
- **1 sweet pepper, thinly sliced**

Mint Dressing
- **½ cup (125 mL) plain yogourt**
- **½ cup (125 mL) sour cream**
- **½ tsp (2.5 mL) paprika**
- **½ tsp (2.5 mL) grated lime rind**
- **2 Tbsp (30 mL) lime juice**
- **2 tsp (10 mL) liquid honey**
- **1 tsp (5 mL) sea salt**
- **1Tbsp (15 mL) fresh mint, washed and finely chopped**

Beans

Steam the beans for 8 minutes or until just tender. Leave to cool.

Whisk the oil, garlic and vinegar in a bowl. Add the beans, green onions and peppers. Marinate for 2 hours or more.

Dressing

Combine all the listed ingredients and blend to a smooth consistency. Serve drizzled over beans.

Makes 4 to 6 servings

Goldie's Kitchen-Sink Salad

Here's a healthy salad you can put together with whatever's in the fridge, cupboard or garden. Toss to coat the salad with some of the dressing and save the rest for another day.

- 3 cups (700 mL) mixed greens, washed and shredded—arugula, kale, spinach, chard or beet greens
- 2 carrots, grated
- 2 stalks celery, chopped
- 1 small onion, 3 green onions or 1 leek, chopped
- ½ cup (125 mL) sprouts—bean sprouts, mixed sprouts or pea shoots
- ¼ cup (60 mL) seeds or nuts— sunflower, pumpkin or hazelnuts
- 1½ cups (350 mL) cooked grain— quinoa, brown rice, bulgur wheat or wheat berries

Dressing
- 1½ lemons, juiced
- 3 garlic cloves, minced
- **2 Tbsp (30 mL) Bragg Liquid Aminos**
- **1 Tbsp (15 mL) nutritional yeast powder**
- **1 Tbsp (15 mL) prepared Dijon mustard or 1 tsp (5 mL) mustard powder**
- 2 tsp (10 mL) liquid honey or maple syrup
- **½ tsp (2.5 mL) black pepper**
- 1 tsp (5 mL) fresh or dried oregano
- **1 cup (250 mL) extra virgin olive oil**

Whisk or blend all the dressing ingredients together, adding the oil last in a slow steady stream until emulsified.

Pour a third of the dressing over the salad and toss well. Save the extra dressing for up to a week in the refrigerator.

Makes 2 servings as a main meal, 6 as a side dish

* if you use maple syrup instead of honey

** if you use brown rice or quinoa

Opposite page: Beet seeds can be direct-seeded in rows, in part sun, come spring or fall. If you grow different varieties you'll have an ongoing harvests of juicy beets—wonderful boiled, roasted, made into soups, pickled or simply grated fresh on salads.

Beet and Orange Salad VG* GF

If you've never tried the combination of beets and oranges, you don't know what you're missing!

1½ lb (700 gr) beets, washed, topped and tailed, greens removed

6 large decorative lettuce or mustard leaves

1 large orange, peeled, sliced thin, chopped into ½-inch (1-cm) triangles

Sprigs of fresh watercress

Dressing

½ cup (125 mL) plain yogourt

2 Tbsp (30 mL) liquid honey

Grated peel and juice of 1 large orange

½ tsp (2.5 mL) fresh-grated nutmeg

1 tsp (5 mL) sea salt

1 tsp (5 mL) fresh-ground black pepper

Cook the beets at a rolling boil for 25 to 30 minutes until they are tender to a knife prick. Drain and cool.

Peel the beets. Cut the peeled beets into ½-inch (1-cm) slices and cut the slices into cubes. Set aside.

Whisk all the dressing ingredients together until well blended.

Fold the beet cubes into the dressing and put into the refrigerator to chill.

Arrange a lettuce or mustard leaf on each of 6 salad plates and place a large spoonful of dressed beets in the centre of each leaf. Garnish with the orange triangles and fresh watercress.

Makes 6 servings

* if you use soy yogourt and maple syrup instead of honey

FALL ENTRÉES

Lobster Mushroom Pasta Bake

I live in a rainforest region, which means that wonderful wild mushrooms are harvested in fall and in plentiful supply September through October. Cooking with wild mushrooms takes me back to dining on porcini in Italy—a taste of Tuscany without the travel!

1 lb (454 gr) whole wheat rotini or penne pasta

3 Tbsp (45 mL) extra virgin olive oil

1 large onion, diced

3 garlic cloves, minced

1 jalapeno pepper, seeds removed, minced

8 oz (225 gr) lobster mushrooms, chopped into ½-inch (1-cm) chunks

1 cob of corn, fresh or frozen, kernels removed

1 bunch Swiss chard, stalks removed, cut into strips

2 tsp (10 mL) ground coarse sea salt

1 tsp (5 mL) fresh-ground pepper

2 fresh tomatoes, chopped

1 cup (250 mL) cheddar cheese, grated

1 cup (250 mL) mozzarella cheese, grated

Preheat oven to 400F (205C).

Cook the pasta in a large saucepan of boiling water until it is al dente in texture, about 10 minutes at a rolling boil.

In a large frying pan, heat the oil and sauté the onion and garlic for about 5 minutes until soft.

Toss the pepper, mushrooms, corn and Swiss chard together with the salt and pepper in a large bowl. Add to the frying pan and sauté for

another 10 minutes over medium heat, until softened.

Add the chopped tomatoes and the cooked pasta. Mix everything together. Pour into a large baking or casserole dish and top with the grated cheese. Reduce the oven heat to 350F (175C) and bake uncovered for 25 minutes, or until the cheese has melted and is lightly browned.

Makes 6 servings

Cabbage and Carrot Stir-Fry

When you're hungry and in a hurry to eat, there's nothing faster than a stir-fry. Whip out your wok for this recipe, and enjoy seriously good fast food!

- 2 Tbsp (30 mL) lemon juice
- 2 Tbsp (30 mL) tamari soy sauce
- 2 Tbsp (30 mL) liquid honey
- 2 Tbsp (30 mL) fresh-grated ginger root
- 1 Tbsp (15 mL) cooking oil—coconut, grapeseed or olive oil
- 1 tsp (5 mL) sesame oil
- 2 garlic cloves, minced
- 6 cups (1.5 L) green cabbage, quartered, cored and shredded
- 2 cups (475 mL) carrots, grated
- 1 tsp (5 mL) gomasio (see page 39)

In a wok, whisk together the lemon juice, soy sauce, honey, ginger, oils and garlic. Heat to boiling.

Toss in the cabbage and carrots and stir-fry over high heat for 5 minutes, stirring occasionally, until the vegetables are lightly crunchy.

Serve sprinkled with gomasio to taste.

Makes 6 servings

* if you use maple syrup

** with gluten-free soy sauce

Fennel, Chard and Goat Cheese Pie

The result is worth the effort when making this recipe. Brushing oil between layers of filo pastry makes it crisp and flaky, and the filling makes it extremely tasty. If your fennel and chard harvest is abundant feel free to double the quantity of filling and make a thicker pie.

2 Tbsp (30 mL) extra virgin olive oil, best quality for best results

1 onion, chopped

3 garlic cloves, minced

1 bulb fennel

1½ tsp (7 mL) sea salt

1 tsp (5 mL) fresh-ground pepper

½ tsp (2.5 mL) chili pepper flakes

1 bunch Swiss chard, leaves shredded and stalks chopped into 1-inch (2.5-cm) pieces

2 tsp (10 mL) Bragg Liquid Aminos

2 large tomatoes, cored and diced

1 bunch fresh parsley, washed and finely chopped

6 oz (170 gr) soft goat cheese

2 eggs, well beaten

1 packet of frozen filo pastry (1 lb/454 gr), thawed

¼ cup (60 mL) extra virgin olive oil for brushing the filo

1 tsp (5 mL) black or white sesame seeds

Preheat oven to 350F (175C).

In a frying pan, heat the olive oil and sauté the onion and garlic for 5 minutes or until soft. Using a mandoline (see page 29) or sharp knife, shave the fennel bulb into thin slices, and add these to the pan together with the salt, pepper and chili pepper flakes. Toss together and sauté for 5 minutes.

Add Bragg's, Swiss chard, tomatoes and parsley. Sauté for another 5 minutes. Using a colander, drain off any liquid or you'll have a soggy pie!

Add the crumbled goat cheese and beaten eggs to the drained mixture and blend all the filling ingredients together well.

Handling carefully so as not to tear, lay 3 sheets of filo pastry over a 9 × 13-inch (23 × 33-cm) oiled baking pan, with the edges of the filo placed over the sides of the pan. Using a pastry brush,

brush the filo lightly with olive oil. Place another filo sheet on top, and lightly brush with olive oil. Repeat these layers 5 more times, brushing oil lightly between each layer.

Spread half the filling over the filo, and cover with 6 more filo sheets, brushing olive oil between each layer, edges placed over the sides of the pan. Spread the remaining half of the filling over the filo, and cover with 6 more filo sheets, brushing oil lightly between each layer.

Fold the pastry edges into the baking pan so that they overlap neatly. Brush olive oil over the very top layer and sprinkle with sesame seeds. Bake in the preheated oven for 30 minutes, or until the pie is golden brown. Allow to sit for 10 minutes before serving.

Makes 8 servings

Ravioli with Garden Tomato Sauce

In fall the garden is bursting with ingredients to create a whole range of ravioli fillings. Fall is wild mushroom season too, and you only need a few fresh chanterelles, lobster or pine mushrooms to make these more gourmet than anything available in the supermarket.

Making homemade ravioli takes time, so it's a perfect activity for a rainy autumn afternoon, while tomato sauce simmers at the back of the stove.

4 cups (1 L) whole wheat flour, sifted to remove rough bran or use half whole wheat and half unbleached white flour*

6 eggs, beaten

3 cups ravioli filling of your choice (see opposite page)

1 batch Garden Tomato Sauce (see opposite page)

Sprigs of basil or Parmigiano-Reggiano to garnish (optional)

Make a well in the flour for the beaten eggs. Using a wooden spoon, slowly draw the flour into the eggs, gradually mixing in more flour until a dough starts to form. Bring the dough together with your hands and knead it into a smooth ball. Allow it to rest for at least 30 minutes at room temperature while you prepare the filling.

Cut the dough into 8 even pieces and form into flattened rectangles. Feed one piece into the pasta machine and roll it through at the widest setting 2 or 3 times to get rid of air bubbles. If the dough rips, fold it in half and roll through again. Reduce the setting and roll again, dusting with a bit of extra flour if things get too sticky. Repeat until the dough is paper thin, but do not go to narrowest setting (check the manufacturer's directions for recommended ravioli setting).

Hang rolled-out dough on a broomstick suspended between two chairs while rolling out the rest—it should start to lose its stickiness, but still be pliable enough to fold without cracking so cover it up if the edges start to dry.

Cut pasta into even squares and place a spoonful of filling in the centre.

Place a square of pasta on top of the filling, and moisten the edges, pushing out any trapped air and crimping the edges together firmly to seal.

Place finished ravioli on a floured counter or in a single layer on a lightly floured parchment-lined tray. They can be cooked immediately or frozen on the tray, then moved into a freezer bag and frozen for up to 3 months.

Cook for approximately 3 to 5 minutes in gently boiling water, until al dente.

Meanwhile, heat the Garden Tomato Sauce in a wide saucepan. Using a large slotted spoon, transfer the cooked ravioli to the saucepan and simmer gently for 5 minutes before serving. A sprig of basil and a grating of Parmigiano-Reggiano cheese provide the perfect finish!

Optional: Filled pasta is also good with a simple topping of olive oil or melted butter with chopped herbs, pepper and salt, and/or grated cheese.

Makes 6 servings

* If you are not experienced at making pasta, use at least half unbleached flour as it makes the dough more pliable and easier to shape.

RAVIOLI FILLING INGREDIENTS

Vegetables: Onions, garlic, mushrooms, spinach, broccoli, chard, kale

Herbs: Dill, oregano, basil, parsley, chives, sweet marjoram, tarragon

Spices: Salt, pepper, chili peppers

Soft Cheeses: Feta, ricotta, soft goat's cheese, fromage fraiche

Hard cheeses: Mozzarella, cheddar, Monterey jack, Parmigiano-Reggiano, Romano, Swiss, fontina

Filling combos

Broccoli florets with sautéed garlic and onions and cheddar

Wild salmon chunks with lemon zest, dill and ricotta cheese

Wild mushrooms with soft goat's cheese and tarragon

Local soft unripened cheeses with steamed and drained garden greens such as kale, chard or spinach, and season with your choice of fresh herb or a dollop of Garlic Scape Pesto (page 150)

Garden Tomato Sauce

At the peak of tomato harvest, we make batches of this sauce, keeping some handy in the fridge, freezing the rest for winter eating. Defrosting a container of sauce in the morning means you can make dinner in 15 minutes. Adding garden vegetables such as zucchini, peppers, onions, carrots or bulb fennel makes a primavera sauce for pasta, pizza or calzones (see page 121).

¼ **cup (60 mL) extra virgin olive oil**

1 **Tbsp (15 mL) garlic, minced**

2 **dried bay leaves**

12 **fresh tomatoes, coarsely chopped**

2 **Tbsp (30 mL) raw cane sugar**

1 **tsp (5 mL) fennel seeds**

1 **tsp (5 mL) black pepper**

1 **tsp (5 mL) sea salt**

1 **tsp (5 mL) ground dried chili peppers, or to taste**

½ **cup (125 mL) fresh parsley, chopped**

½ **cup (125 mL) fresh basil, chopped**

Heat the oil and sizzle the garlic for a few minutes without browning. Add the bay leaves. Add the tomatoes, sugar and seasonings, except for the fresh herbs, parsley and basil. Reduce heat to low and leave to simmer for 2½ hours, or until *thickened. Stir in the chopped parsley and basil at the end.*

Makes 2 cups (475 mL)

Fall Desserts

Are Melons Ripe?

Melons are best harvested ripe from the garden, but how can you tell? It's actually quite easy and there are a number of signs to look for:

- Try the basic "thump" test. Thump the melon—if it sounds hollow, it's most likely ripe.
- Check the colour of the spot where the melon sat on the ground. If it is white or pale green, the melon is not ripe yet. If it's yellow or cream, the melon is ripe.
- Look for a dulling of the skin, which happens as the melon reaches maturity.
- Check the stem attachment. Cantaloupes and muskmelons are at peak flavour when the stem becomes "corky" so that the fruit slips easily off the vine.
- Look at the tendril on the melon vine. If it has turned brown and begun to dry, the melon's ripe. Melons store best if kept at 50F (10C).

IF YOU GIVE A FIG...

"Nectar from the Gods" is the way I describe eating ripe figs plucked from the tree and warm from the sun. There are so many ways to enjoy them:

- Add chopped fresh figs to fruit salads.
- Poach fresh figs in red wine and serve drizzled with cream.
- Add quartered figs to a salad of thinly sliced bulb fennel, arugula leaves and shaved Parmigiano-Reggiano cheese.
- Make exquisite hors d'oeuvres by stuffing fresh figs with cream cheese mixed with finely chopped nuts.

This Chanteray melon from Foxglove Farm on Salt Spring Island was plucked off the vine at peak ripeness.

Apple Nut Bars

Apples that retain texture when cooked, such as 'Bramley' cooking apples, work best here.

Pastry

1 cup (250 mL) salted butter, chilled

2½ cups (600 mL) unbleached white flour (or half whole wheat and half unbleached white)

1 egg yolk, beaten (save egg white for brushing pastry at the end)

⅓ cup (80 mL) cold milk

Filling

4 cups (1 L) peeled, cored and thinly sliced cooking apples, (see Apple Peeler, page 32)

1 cup (250 mL) raw cane sugar

2 Tbsp (30 mL) unbleached white flour or half white and half whole wheat flour

2 Tbsp (30 mL) butter

½ tsp (2.5 mL) cinnamon powder

1 cup (250 mL) hazelnuts or almonds, ground

Topping

1 egg white, whisked

1 tsp (5 mL) cinnamon

1 tsp (5 mL) raw cane sugar

Pastry

Using a pastry blender or 2 knives, cut the butter into the flour to form a coarse, crumbly texture. Mix the egg with the milk and stir it in using a fork until the pastry comes together. Using your hands, form a ball, handling it as little as possible.

Cut the ball into 2, and roll each half into a sheet of even thickness to fit a 9 × 13-inch (23 × 33-cm) baking pan. Place 1 sheet on the bottom of the baking pan right up to the edges. Put in the refrigerator to chill as you make the filling.

Filling

Mix all the filling ingredients together except for the ground nuts. Sprinkle ½ cup (125 mL) of the nuts over the pastry sheet in the baking pan.

Spread the filling evenly over the pan, and dot with butter. Sprinkle the remaining ½ cup (125 mL) nuts over the top.

Cover this filling with the remaining sheet of pastry, crimping edges together with your fingers or a fork. Beat the egg white with the cinnamon and 1 tsp (5 mL) sugar, and use a pastry brush to brush this mix evenly over the pastry. Prick with a fork in several places to release steam while baking.

Reduce oven temperature to 350F (175C) and bake for 30 minutes until golden brown. Allow to cool before cutting into bars for serving or storing refrigerated between layers of wax paper.

Makes 12 large bars

Aunt Minnie's Cherry Cake

This cake is so moist and scrumptious that I'd wager a bet you'll want another piece! You can use any fruit with this recipe—blueberries, strawberries, mixed berries, apples or pears.

1 Tbsp (15 mL) butter

3 Tbsp (45 mL) black or white sesame seeds

1 cup (250 mL) brown sugar

1¼ cups (300 mL) vegetable oil

3 eggs, beaten

2 tsp (10 mL) pure vanilla extract

1½ cup (350 mL) unbleached white flour

1½ cup (350 mL) whole wheat flour

1 tsp (5 mL) baking soda

1 tsp (5 mL) baking powder

¼ tsp (1 mL) ground cardamom

1 tsp (5 mL) cinnamon powder

3 cups (700 mL) cherries (TIP: If using frozen fruit, thaw first and drain off any liquid)

1 cup (250 mL) nuts, finely chopped— hazelnuts, pecans or walnuts

Preheat the oven to 350F (175C).

Butter a 9 × 13-inch (23 × 33-cm) baking pan. Sprinkle the sesame seeds evenly over the sides and base.

Beat the sugar and oil together until smooth. Beat the eggs with the vanilla and add gradually to the sugar mixture until it becomes smooth.

Sift the flours with the leavening agents and spices.

Add the dry ingredients to the wet, beating with a wooden spoon until the batter is smooth. Fold the fruit and nuts into the batter with the wooden spoon.

Scoop the batter into the prepared baking pan with a spatula, smoothing it into the edges.

Place in the oven and bake for 45 minutes, checking for browning after 30 minutes. If the top is too brown, place some foil over the cake as it bakes for the last 15 minutes. Check doneness with a toothpick in the centre of the cake—if done it will come out clean.

Makes 12 servings

Poached Pears VG* GF

These make a light and delectable dessert, but for a gourmet delight, add chopped poached pears to a mixed-greens salad with some roasted nuts and strong blue cheese. Strain the poaching liquid through a cheesecloth-lined sieve to remove the spices and enjoy hot mulled wine for your trouble! Make this dish ahead of time so that there is time to chill it.

6 perfectly ripe pears, peeled and cored

3¼ cups (750 mL) red wine

4 cups (1 L) water

1 lemon, cut in half

½ cup (125 mL) honey

1-inch (2.5-cm) piece of fresh ginger root

½ tsp (2.5 mL) whole cloves

2 star anise

1 bay leaf

Place the pears in a large saucepan and add the rest of the ingredients, so that the pears are covered in the poaching liquid. Bring to the boil, then reduce the heat to a low simmer and cook for 25 minutes.

Remove the pears from the liquid with a slotted spoon and refrigerate for 4 hours or overnight. Serve chilled.

Makes 6 servings

* if you use maple syrup

Granny's Plum Kuchen

My granny passed this recipe onto my mother and thankfully she passed it on to me. This elegant sweet and sour streusel plum tart is a "five-star dessert" according to friends, who never resist a second piece. The secret to success lies in the variety of plums—choose sweeter fleshy plums rather than juicy ones that can make the tart too moist. Do I need to mention whipped cream?

1 cup (250 mL) butter, chilled

1 cup (250 mL) plus 2 Tbsp (30 mL) granulated white sugar

2 ²/₃ cups (630 mL) unbleached white flour, plus ½ cup (125 mL) extra for coating

2 large eggs

1 lb (450 gr) 'Damson' or prune plums, halved, stones removed

1 Tbsp (15 mL) raw cane or brown sugar

1 tsp (5 mL) cinnamon powder

Zest of 1 lemon

Preheat oven to 400F (205C).

Chop chunks of cold butter into a large mixing bowl. Add the white sugar and 2 ²/₃ cup (630 mL) flour. Using a pastry cutter or 2 knives, chop the butter into the flour mix until it just starts to form a coarse crumb texture. Now, using your fingertips, work the coarser texture into a more uniform crumble. Beat eggs with a whisk and pour over the flour mixture in the bowl. Using a fork, stir in circles until a moist crumble forms. Sprinkle the remaining ½ cup (125 mL) flour over the moist crumbs in the bowl to coat them.

Pour two-thirds of this mixture into a 12-inch (30-cm) spring-form pan. Using your fingers, press evenly over the bottom and 2 inches (5 cm) up the sides of the pan.

Put the plums in a separate bowl and sprinkle with the brown sugar, lemon zest and cinnamon. Gently toss together so that the plums are well coated. Pour the plums over the crumble base in the pan. Spread the remaining third of the crumble evenly over the plums, finally tapping the pan gently on the counter to level crumbs right up to the edge.

Reduce the oven to 350F (175C) and bake for 45 minutes. After the first 30 minutes, check the top for browning and cover with foil if necessary to complete baking.

Leave to cool before removing the sides of the spring-form pan and serving.

Makes 12 servings

FALL DRINKS

Apple Tea `VG*` `GF`

This nutritious tea has a surprisingly irresistible flavour, and the resulting poached apples are good, too. The tea is also a soothing remedy for winter chills and fevers.

- 3 large apples, cored and sliced, but not peeled
- **3 cups (700 mL) cold water, filtered if necessary**
- **2 cups (475 mL) boiling water**
- 1 tsp (5 mL) fresh lemon juice
- 1 tsp (5 mL) honey

Put the apple slices and the cold water into a large Mason jar. Cover with the snap lid and secure with the metal ring.

Boil 2 cups (475 mL) water in a saucepan, and set the jar into the water. Leave to simmer gently over low heat for 2 hours.

Remove from the heat. Strain the poached apples through a fine-mesh sieve. Stir the lemon juice and honey into the liquid, and enjoy sipping the apple tea while it is still hot.

Makes 3 cups (700 mL)

* if you use maple syrup instead of honey

Herbal Espresso

Chicory and dandelion roots can be wildcrafted fresh or purchased already roasted from herbal-remedy stores. And pearl barley can be purchased in bulk from local health food stores. This is a truly delicious drink that can help you to get off the caffeine kick—and this from a coffee aficionado!

- **1 cup (250 mL) chicory root, roasted**
- **¼ cup (60 mL) dandelion root, roasted**
- **¼ cup (60 mL) pearl barley, roasted**

Preheat oven to 275F (135C).

Roasting chicory and dandelion roots

Scrub, but do not peel the roots. Cut out any bad bits or ingrained dirt that cannot be removed. Pat dry using a teacloth. Chop the roots into ½-inch (1-cm) chunks and place on a baking sheet (not oiled). Reduce the heat in the oven to 200F (95C) and roast the roots, turning every 10 minutes or so for even roasting.

Roasting pearl barley

Heat a frying pan or griddle to medium-high heat. Pour in the pearl barley and shake over the heat for about 10 minutes, as the barley roasts and becomes lightly browned.

Making "coffee"

Grind the above ingredients in a coffee grinder to the same consistency you would coffee for a French press. Store the herbal espresso in a sealed glass jar out of sunlight. TIP: Do not over-grind this mixture to powder because it will clog the plunger in your French press.

French Press Mocha Espresso

Make this latte-style, using a glass frother (about $20 from your local kitchen store) and a 1 L carafe French press.

- **⅓ cup (80 mL) soy milk**
- **3 Tbsp (45 mL) herbal espresso (see above)**
- **1 tsp (5 mL) carob or cacao powder**
- **1 cup (250 mL) boiling water**
- **2 tsp (10 mL) maple syrup**
- **Dash cinnamon powder**
- **1 cup (250 mL) boiling water**

Heat the soy milk to just below boiling. Do not allow to boil. Pour the warmed milk into the frother to the mark indicated, and plunge until the frother is filled to the top with creamy foamed milk.

Put the herbal espresso and carob or cocoa into a French press and add the boiling water and maple syrup. Stir then plunge.

Fill 4 coffee cups one-third full with the espresso, then top up with creamy foam. Sprinkle with cinnamon.

Makes 4 servings

WINTER

WINTER RECIPES

Creamy Parsnip and Apple Soup VG* GF

Parsnips and apples make a great team for your taste buds. Try this smooth and creamy soup to find out for yourself!

2 Tbsp (30 mL) vegetable oil

1 large onion, chopped

2 tsp (10 mL) brown sugar

2 cups (475 mL) parsnips, peeled and chopped

1½ cups (350 mL) potatoes, scrubbed and diced

4 cups (1 L) Vegetable Stock with Lovage (see page 60)

2 cups (475 mL) apple juice

4 apples, peeled, cored and chopped

1 Tbsp (15 mL) freshly squeezed lemon juice

1 tsp (5 mL) ground cinnamon

¼ tsp (1 mL) sea salt

½ tsp (2.5 mL) fresh-ground black pepper

½ tsp (2.5 mL) grated whole nutmeg

1 cup (250 mL) milk or cream (optional for creamier soup)

Heat the oil in a large saucepan and add the onion with the brown sugar. Sauté for 10 minutes over low-medium heat, allowing the onion to caramelize a little.

Add the parsnips and potatoes to the softened onions along with the vegetable stock and apple juice. Bring to the boil, reduce heat and cover. Simmer for 20 minutes.

Add the apples, lemon juice and seasonings to the saucepan. Simmer for another 20 minutes.

Purée the soup in a food blender until smooth, and return it to the saucepan.

Whisk in milk or cream if desired. Season with fresh-grated nutmeg.

Makes 10 servings

* if you use soy milk or cream

Russian Beet Borscht VG* GF

This hearty seasonal soup is delicious served with Cheesy Corn Bread (page 192), and is even tastier the following day. I often throw a bag of tomatoes from the freezer into it for added flavour.

2 Tbsp (30 mL) extra virgin olive oil

1 large onion, chopped

1 bunch (6–8) beets with greens, washed, stalks removed

8 cups (2 L) water

3 carrots, diced

6 medium potatoes, diced

1 dried bay leaf

2 tsp (10 mL) fresh or 1 tsp (5 mL) dried dill

2 Tbsp (30 mL) apple cider vinegar

1 Tbsp (15 mL) honey

1 cup (250 mL) Tomato Paste (see page 73)

6 fresh tomatoes, chopped

2 tsp (10 mL) fresh-ground black pepper

2 tsp (10 mL) sea salt

Garnishes: Parsley, chives

Optional garnish: yogourt

Heat the olive oil in a large frying pan, and sauté the onion until soft, about 5 minutes. Shred the beet greens into 1-inch (2.5-cm) strips, add to the frying pan and sauté until just softened. Set the pan aside.

In a large saucepan, add the water and the whole beets, and cook for about 25 minutes until the beets are tender. Using a slotted spoon, remove the beets and leave them to cool. When cool, dice them approximately the same size as the potatoes and carrots.

Add the carrots, potatoes, diced beets and bay leaf to the beet cooking water and bring to the boil. Reduce heat and simmer for about 15 minutes, until the vegetables are just tender. Blend in the sautéed greens and onions and all the rest of the ingredients. Cook over low to medium heat for another 15 minutes to allow flavours to meld.

Garnish with parsley and/or chives sprinkled over yogourt if you like.

Makes 10 servings

* if you use maple syrup instead of honey, and skip the yogourt

Miso Seaweed Soup VG GF*

I am fortunate to live on an island surrounded by pristine beaches from which many species of edible seaweeds are harvested. I include these in my zero-mile diet as a wonderful source of minerals. See Sea Vegetables (page 47).

Miso is a high-protein seasoning made from soybeans, cultured grain, salt and water. It's very versatile and great for soups, sauces, dips, gravies and dressings. Amano Genmai Miso is a naturally aged and gluten-free blend of organic brown rice, organic soybeans (non-GM), sea salt and filtered water. The bran of the rice kernel adds a rich brown colour to the nutty flavour of this miso. Miso should be kept refrigerated.

8 cups (2 L) water

1 large leek or 6 green onions, finely sliced

1 large carrot, grated

3 large fresh mushrooms, thinly sliced (see Mandoline, page 29) or use dried mushrooms such as shiitake

3 garlic cloves, minced

1-inch (2.5-cm) fresh ginger root, finely chopped

3 Tbsp (45 mL) miso

8 oz (225 gr) firm tofu, diced into ¼–½-inch (5 mm–1 cm) cubes

12 inches (30 cm) of dried kelp or wakame seaweed, cut into 1-inch (2.5-cm) pieces (scissors work best)

1 Tbsp tamari soy sauce

Garnish with minced parsley or fresh coriander leaves (optional)

Fill a large saucepan with the water and add all the vegetables, garlic and ginger. Bring the water to the boil, reduce the heat and simmer gently for 10 minutes.

Stir the miso with a ½ cup (125 mL) of the hot soup water to make a smooth paste, and then incorporate this paste into the soup. Do not allow the soup to boil. Add the tofu cubes, the seaweed pieces and tamari soy sauce to taste.

Simmer for another 5 minutes before serving.

Makes 8 to 10 servings

* with gluten-free soy sauce.

Amber's Vegan Pâté VG GF*

This spicy pâté is delicious as an appetizer with crackers, but we also enjoy eating it for dinner, accompanied by a salad.

- ½ **cup (125 mL) whole wheat, buckwheat, soy or bean flour**
- ½ **cup (125 mL) nutritional yeast**
- 1 **tsp (5 mL) dried thyme**
- 1 **tsp (5 mL) dried sage**
- 1 **tsp (5 mL) dried savory**
- 1 **tsp (5 mL) sea salt**
- 1 **tsp (5 mL) fresh-ground black pepper**
- 1 **tsp (5 mL) dry mustard powder**
- 1 **tsp (5 mL) ground dried chili peppers**
- 1 **cup (250 mL) sunflower seeds**
- 1 **large carrot, grated**
- 1 **onion, chopped small**
- 2 **garlic cloves, minced**
- 1 **stalk celery, chopped small**
- 1 **potato, peeled and diced small**
- 1 **cup (250 mL) water**
- ½ **cup (125 mL) vegetable oil**
- 2 **Tbsp (30 mL) fresh lemon juice**

Preheat oven to 350F (175C).

In a large bowl, blend all the dry ingredients and seasonings together well.

Prepare the vegetables and mix them and the sunflower seeds with the dry ingredients already in the bowl.

Add the wet ingredients, stirring thoroughly and blending well.

Using a spatula, spread the pâté evenly into an 8-inch (20-cm) square baking dish.

Place the dish in the preheated oven and bake for 1 hour. When done, it will be firm to the touch and lightly browned.

Makes 12 servings as an appetizer, or 4 servings as a main course

* if you replace wheat flour with buckwheat, soy or bean flour

Crispy Kale Chips VG* GF**

When baked, kale turns crispy and unlike potato chips, kale chips are low in fat and easy to make at home. Choose a coarse kale such as 'Lacinato', green or purple curly kale. Each variety provides a different eating experience.

1 bunch kale, washed and dried, ribs removed, torn into bite-sized pieces

Dressing

2 Tbsp (30 mL) peanut butter, tahini or other nut butter of choice

1 Tbsp (15 mL) tamari soy sauce

1 Tbsp (15 mL) apple cider vinegar

1 Tbsp (15 mL) extra virgin olive oil

2 Tbsp (30 mL) hot water

½ tsp (2.5 mL) liquid honey or maple syrup

½ tsp (2.5 mL) grated ginger root

½ tsp (2.5 mL) sesame seeds

In a blender, food processor or bowl with a whisk, blend the dressing ingredients.

Preheat oven to 325F (160C).

In a large bowl, toss the kale leaves with dressing until evenly coated and arrange in a single layer on a baking sheet lined with parchment. Use two baking sheets or cook in batches if needed—the chips won't cook evenly if the leaves overlap.

Place the sheet in the middle of the preheated oven and bake for 10 minutes. Using tongs (or your fingers), turn the leaves over and bake for another 10 to 15 minutes until the kale is crispy,

but not burnt. Keep an eye on it and remove any finished chips before they become overcooked. They should be dry, but should not shatter to the touch.

Cool briefly then eat right away—they won't stay crispy for long, but don't worry, they disappear quickly!

Makes 4 servings

* *if you use maple syrup*

** *with gluten-free soy sauce*

Yule Log

Place this festive yule log on a handsome platter, decorate it with a sprig of holly and serve with assorted crackers and mulled spice wine (page 249).

4 oz (112 gr) cream cheese, softened

4 oz (112 gr) soft goat's cheese, plain

1 Tbsp (15 mL) dried fines herbs (choose from tarragon, chervil, chives, parsley or sweet marjoram) or 1 Tbsp (15 mL) Fines Herbes Salées du Bas-du-Fleuve (see page 58)

½ cup (125 mL), hazelnuts, almonds or walnuts, lightly toasted and finely chopped

In a small bowl, blend the cheeses and herbs together. Cover and refrigerate to allow the flavours to meld and to make it easier to handle.

To toast nuts

Preheat the oven to 300F (150C).

Spread the nuts on a baking sheet and place in the oven for 10 to 15 minutes or until lightly browned. Shake the pan every 5 minutes to turn the nuts for even roasting. TIP: Use a timer. It's easy to forget them!

Shape the chilled cheese into a log shape. Spread the finely chopped nuts out on a board, and roll the log over them until evenly coated on all sides.

Makes 8 to 10 servings

White Bean Vegan Dip VG GF

This is an easy-to-prepare, nutritious and tasty dip. Garnish with a fresh sprig of rosemary and serve with chunks of warm rustic bread, vegetable sticks or crackers.

1 bulb roasted garlic (see page 31)

2 cups (475 mL) white cannellini or navy beans, cooked

2 Tbsp (30 mL) extra virgin olive oil

1 tsp (5 mL) rosemary, finely chopped

½ tsp (2.5 mL) sea salt

½ tsp (2.5 mL) fresh-ground black pepper

Squeeze the roasted garlic into the bowl of a food processor.

Add the cooked beans, olive oil, rosemary, salt and pepper.

Blend into a smooth paste. Chill before serving.

Makes 6 to 8 servings

Krunchy Kale Salad VG GF*

This nutritious salad recipe is a keeper because Kathleen makes it for Jeanie's 18-month-old twins, and says they can't get enough of it! Make the salad a couple of hours in advance so that it can chill before serving.

¼ cup (60 mL) pumpkin seeds

¼ cup (60 mL) sunflower seeds

1 Tbsp (15 mL) tamari soy sauce

½ head red cabbage, core removed, thinly sliced

1 bunch kale, ribs removed, thinly sliced

3 cups (700 mL) carrots, grated

Dressing

½ cup (125 mL) extra virgin olive oil

¼ cup (60 mL) Bragg Liquid Aminos

3 Tbsp (45 mL) balsamic vinegar

2 tsp (10 mL) dried oregano

Toast the seeds in a cast-iron skillet or frying pan over medium heat, shaking occasionally until lightly browned. Add the soy sauce and sizzle for a minute or so. Remove from the heat and allow the seeds to cool.

In a large bowl, combine all the vegetables and add the toasted seeds.

Dressing

In a small bowl, whisk together the dressing ingredients.

Toss the salad with the dressing until it is evenly coated and leave to chill for 2 hours before serving. Keeps refrigerated for up to 3 days.

Makes 10 to 12 servings

* with gluten-free soy sauce

Winter Side Dishes

Sweet and Sour Red Cabbage `VG*` `GF`

In our family home, it was traditional for my mother to serve this tasty cabbage dish at Christmas with Brussels sprouts. However, it's so good I think you'll want to make it at other times, too.

- 1½ lb (700 gr) medium-sized red cabbage, cored and sliced
- 2 apples, cored and chopped
- 2 medium onions, chopped
- 3 garlic cloves, chopped
- ¼ cup (60 mL) vegetable oil
- ¼ cup (60 mL) honey
- 1 cup (250 mL) hot water
- ½ cup (125 mL) red wine vinegar
- ½ cup (125 mL) raisins
- 1 tsp (5 mL) sea salt
- 1 tsp (5 mL) fresh-ground black pepper

Put all the ingredients into a slow cooker or a large stainless-steel saucepan.

Simmer over low to medium heat for 3 to 4 hours, *or until the cabbage is juicy, sweet and tender. Keeps well refrigerated.*

Makes 6 servings

* if you use maple syrup instead of honey

Squash, Sunchoke and Potato Roast VG GF

I love veggie roasts. They are fast to throw together, take no effort to cook and are so tasty. You can make use of whatever vegetables you have handy at the time: parsnips, celeriac, potatoes, squash, sunchokes…all make good roasting ingredients! And here's one delicious variation.

2 apples, quartered and cored
10 small potatoes
10 sunchoke tubers
1 small butternut squash, peeled and chopped
½ cup (125 mL) dried berries—goji berries, cranberries, etc.
Sprig of rosemary, needles only
1 tsp (5 mL) dried sage
1 tsp (5 mL) coarse salt
1 tsp (5 mL) fresh-ground pepper
Drizzle of grapeseed oil
Splash of balsamic vinegar
Drizzle of maple syrup

Preheat oven to 350F (175C).

Toss all the ingredients together on a baking pan and roast in the preheated oven for 45 minutes.

Makes 4 to 6 servings

Another colourful medley for your dinner table—make as many servings as you need by using more vegetables. Combine bite-sized pieces of turnip, beet, carrot, potato, onion and bulb fennel in a single layer on a baking sheet. Drizzle with olive oil and sprinkle with salt and pepper. Bake in a 350F (175C) oven until tender.

Harvest squash before hard frost.

Goldie's Quince and Sunchoke Roast VG GF

You'll be surprised how tasty this combination of flavours is.

- **4 quince, quartered and cored**
- **4 large sunchokes, scrubbed clean**
- **4 large potatoes, scrubbed clean, not peeled**
- **2 tsp (10 mL) dried sage**
- **1 tsp (5 mL) sea salt**
- **1 tsp (5 mL) fresh-ground black pepper**
- **½ cup (125 mL) extra virgin olive oil**
- **¼ cup (60 mL) maple syrup**

Preheat oven to 350F (175C).

Cut the vegetables into approximately same-sized chunks.

Mix in the seasonings, drizzle with the olive oil and toss until covered.

Roast in the preheated oven for 30 minutes.

Drizzle with maple syrup when the dish comes out of the oven and serve.

Makes 4 servings

Sunchoke Casserole `VG` `GF`

Who knew that sunchokes could make such a delicious casserole? Surprise your dinner guests by serving this dish and asking them to guess the main ingredient. Then you can also turn them on to all the wonderful possibilities of enjoying sunchokes.

2 Tbsp (60 mL) extra virgin olive oil

1 medium onion, chopped

2 garlic cloves, minced

1½ lb (700 gr) sunchokes, thinly sliced (see Mandoline, page 29)

½ tsp (2.5 mL) fresh-grated nutmeg

1 tsp (5 mL) sweet basil

1 tsp (5 mL) sweet marjoram

1 tsp (5 mL) salt

1 tsp (5 mL) pepper

4 fresh tomatoes, chopped

½ cup (125 mL) dry red wine

½ cup (125 mL) water

Preheat oven to 350F (175C).

Heat the oil in a large frying pan and sauté the onion and garlic for 5 minutes until soft. Add the sliced sunchokes, nutmeg, herbs, salt and pepper. Sauté for another 10 minutes.

Place in a casserole dish, and toss with the tomatoes, wine and water. Cover and bake for 1 hour until the liquid has evaporated.

Makes 4 servings

Sunchoke Tips

Sunchokes, or Jerusalem artichokes, are a blessing all winter, because these knobby tubers can be dug from the garden as needed, and the flavour is enhanced by hard frosts. Here's what you should know about using them in the kitchen:

- They have the best nutrition when eaten fresh. To prepare sunchokes, scrub them clean using a vegetable brush—it's best not to peel them, because most of the nutrient content is just under the skin.
- Once sunchokes are cut, they will discolour, so cut them close to serving time, or immerse them in cold water with lemon juice or vinegar to prevent oxidation and discolouring.

- To store tubers, wrap them in a plastic bag. They will keep up to two weeks in the refrigerator.

RAW SUNCHOKES

Enjoy the crunch of raw sunchokes added to salads, or serve with crudités and dips. Try grating sunchokes into coleslaw with carrots and cabbage.

SUNCHOKE SALAD

Scrub and wash the sunchokes and put into a pot of cold salted water. Simmer until just tender for 10 minutes. Slice them while they are still warm. Season with a drizzle of olive oil, white wine vinegar or lemon juice, parsley, minced garlic, salt and pepper. Allow to chill for a tasty salad.

ROAST SUNCHOKES

In a bowl, toss whole cleaned sunchokes with extra virgin olive oil and season with sea salt and pepper to taste. Place on a baking sheet or in a garlic roaster (see page 31) and bake at 375F (190C) for 30 minutes, turning to recoat with oil halfway through. The flavour will become agreeably sweet and nutty. Serve them as you would roast potatoes.

Sunchoke and potato purée

Scrub sunchoke tubers and an equal amount of potatoes, and chop into same-sized chunks. Put the chunks into a steam basket over a saucepan filled with boiling water. Cover and steam for about 10 minutes until soft. Mash as you would boiled potatoes, and season with parsley, fresh-grated whole nutmeg, and salt and pepper to taste.

In winter, sunchoke tubers are dug directly from the garden as required. Front: Oca (New Zealand yam). Middle left: Red sunchokes. Middle right: Crosnes (Chinese artichokes). Rear left: White sunchokes. These can be boiled, baked, roasted or deep-fried, like potatoes.

WINTER ENTRÉES

Cranberry Panini Sandwich

My friend Mark told me that whenever he makes this panini sandwich people ask for the recipe. So naturally I asked to put it in my cookbook! A panini grill can be bought for about $60—worth every penny when you get creative with all the amazing sandwich fillings possible. If you don't own a grill, you can also cook this sandwich in a waffle iron, on a cast-iron griddle or frying pan with a heat-proof weight on top—you just don't get the stripey effect!

Focaccia or ciabatta
Cranberry Spread (see recipe below)
Portobello mushroom, thinly sliced
Fresh and tender asparagus spears (optional)
A few leaves of arugula or mixed winter greens
Brie cheese, thinly sliced

Slice a slab of focaccia or ciabatta in half, and spread each half with a layer of cranberry spread.

Layer the mushroom, asparagus, arugula and cheese on top of one half, and put the other half of the bread on top.

Place on a preheated panini grill, and cook for 5 minutes or until the brie has melted and the bread is nicely browned.

Makes 1 sandwich

Cranberry Spread

2 Tbsp (30 mL) butter
1 large sweet onion, peeled and diced
1 Tbsp (15 mL) balsamic vinegar
1 Tbsp (15 mL) brown cane sugar
1 cup (250 mL) dried cranberries
1 tsp (5 mL) cinnamon powder

Melt the butter in a small saucepan and sauté the onion for about 5 minutes until soft, and then add the vinegar and sugar. Sauté over low to medium heat to caramelize the onions.

Add the cranberries and cinnamon and simmer over low heat for 10 minutes. Leave to cool and blend until smooth in a food processor.

Makes 1 cup (250 mL)

Beet Burgers

These burgers are delicious topped with sauce and eaten in a bun with sprouts. Freeze extras between sheets of waxed paper and cook as needed.

¼ cup (60 mL) vegetable oil

2 large eggs

2 Tbsp (30 mL) tamari soy sauce or Bragg Liquid Aminos

2 cups (475 mL) whole beets, grated

2 cups (475 mL) carrots, grated

1 large onion, diced

3 garlic cloves, minced

2 cups (475 mL) cooked quinoa or brown rice

1 cup (250 mL) cheddar cheese, grated

½ cup (125 mL) toasted sunflower seeds

½ cup (125 mL) whole wheat flour

3 Tbsp (45 mL) fresh dill or 1 Tbsp (15 mL) dried dill

Sauce

1 cup (250 mL) plain yogourt

¼ cup (60 mL) mayonnaise (see Free-Range Egg Mayonnaise, page 157)

3 Tbsp (45 mL) Tomato Paste (see page 73)

Dash of hot sauce or cayenne pepper to taste

Preheat oven to 350F (175C).

In a large bowl, beat the oil, eggs and soy sauce together. Combine this mixture thoroughly with the vegetables, garlic, grains, cheese, seeds, flour and dill.

Shape ½ cup (125 mL) of the mixture into patties about ¾ inch (2 cm) thick.

Space the patties on a greased baking sheet.

Place the sheet in the preheated oven, and bake for 20 minutes on one side. Turn them over and bake for another 25 minutes.

Makes 10 burgers

Bean and Cheese Burrito

These are wonderful eaten with hot sauce (see page 120).

- **½ cup (125 mL) refried beans (below)**
- **½ cup (125 mL) cooked quinoa or rice**
- **Grated Monterey jack, cheddar or mozzarella cheese to taste**
- **1 large whole grain tortilla**

Preheat oven to 350F (175C).

Spread a dollop of refried beans, together with quinoa or rice and some grated cheese (Monterey jack, cheddar or mozzarella), over a whole grain tortilla. Fold in the edges, roll up tightly and place on a baking sheet. Cover with foil and bake in a 350F (175C) oven for 15 minutes until the cheese melts.

Makes 1 serving

* with a gluten-free tortilla

Refried Beans VG GF

Once beans are cooked, you can easily turn them into tasty refried beans that can be eaten as a side dish or added to wraps and burritos with other ingredients.

- **2 cups (475 mL) cooked pinto beans (see Easy Slow Cooker Beans, page 38)**
- **2 tsp (10 mL) sea salt**
- **1 bunch fresh cilantro, minced**
- **1 lime, juiced**

Put the beans and other seasonings in a frying pan, and mash them in the liquid using a potato masher.

Cook the refried beans over medium heat just enough to get the required consistency.

Makes 2 cups (475 mL)

Thai Squash Stew VG GF

This satisfying Thai stew is first prepared in a wok, and then left to simmer in a slow cooker. Serve on top of brown rice garnished with fresh leaves of cilantro or Thai basil.

½ cup (125 mL) blanched almonds*

3 Tbsp (45 mL) vegetable oil

½ tsp (2.5 mL) ground cumin seed

1 tsp (5 mL) ground coriander seed

½ tsp (2.5 mL) turmeric powder

½ tsp (2.5 mL) ground fennel seed

2-inch (5-cm) chunk of ginger root, peeled and finely chopped

2 lb (908 gr) butternut squash, seeded, peeled, chopped into 1-inch (2.5-cm) pieces

2 stalks celery or 1 fennel bulb, sliced thinly

2 medium carrots, sliced thinly

1 fresh or dried jalapeno pepper, seeded

½ cup (125 mL) water

14 oz (398 mL) can coconut milk

1 tsp (5 mL) sea salt

8 oz (225 gr) tofu, rinsed, cut into 2 × ½-inch (5 × 1-cm) strips

Garnish: Fresh cilantro

Spread 1 tsp (5 mL) vegetable oil over a frying pan or griddle. Toast the almonds, shaking often, until lightly browned. Set aside.

Heat the remaining oil in a wok. Add the spices and the ginger and warm for a few minutes to release their aromas. Add all the vegetables and water and sauté together with the spices for 5 minutes over medium-high heat.

Stir in the coconut milk and the salt. Pour into a slow cooker. Cook on medium-low heat for 2 hours, stirring occasionally if you are around.

Add the tofu strips and blanched and roasted almonds to the slow cooker, and finish stewing for another 20 minutes.

Makes 6 servings

* To blanch almonds, boil 1 cup (250 mL) water and add the whole almonds. Leave to stand for 2 minutes. Drain. Slip off the skins and spread the almonds out until they have dried.

JACKIE'S CURRIED FEAST

I always look forward to dinner at Jackie's home because she puts her soul into her cooking, so it tastes wonderful! This is the feast Jackie prepared last time we were invited over, served with Rhubarb Ginger Chutney (see page 85).

Curried Squash and Lentils VG* GF

- 1 Tbsp (15 mL) butter or oil
- 3 garlic cloves, minced
- 1 tsp (5 mL) ground coriander
- 1 tsp (5 mL) ground cumin
- 1 tsp (5 mL) turmeric
- ¼ tsp (1 mL) cayenne pepper, powdered
- ½ tsp (2.5 mL) ground cloves
- ½ tsp (2.5 mL) ground cinnamon
- ½ tsp (2.5 mL) ground ginger
- 1 tsp (5 mL) sea salt
- 2 cups (475 mL) cooked brown lentils, with the reserved cooking liquid
- 1 medium squash or pumpkin, peeled, seeded and diced into ½-inch (1-cm) chunks
- 2 Tbsp (30 mL) fresh lemon juice
- 1 tomato, diced
- 1 Tbsp (15 mL) fresh cilantro, chopped

Melt the butter and add the minced garlic and all the spices, allowing them to release their aromas.

Stir in the cooked lentils and the diced squash, with enough of the reserved liquid to cover. Cook over medium heat for about 30 minutes, stirring, until the squash is tender.

Stir in the lemon juice, tomato and chopped cilantro. Taste and adjust seasoning if needed.

Makes 4 to 6 servings

Curried Potatoes and Cabbage

3 Tbsp (45 mL) vegetable oil

1 tsp (5 mL) crushed red chili pepper

½ tsp (2.5 mL) ground ginger

½ tsp (2.5 mL) whole mustard seeds

½ tsp (2.5 mL) ground cumin

2 dried bay leaves

1 tsp (5 mL) ground coriander

½ tsp (2.5 mL) turmeric powder

2 tsp (10 mL) sea salt

1 medium cabbage, 2.2 lb (1 kg), coarsely shredded

6 large potatoes, diced into ½-inch (1-cm) cubes

1 cup (250 mL) water

1 Tbsp (15 mL) butter

½ tsp (2.5 mL) garam masala (see page 241)

1 Tbsp (15 mL) lemon juice

½ tsp (2.5 mL) raw cane sugar

Heat the oil in a skillet and toast the spices for 2 minutes, stirring constantly. Add the shredded cabbage and potato. Stir until coated with the spices and sauté for 10 to 15 minutes. Add water, cover and cook for 20 minutes over medium heat.

Add the butter, garam masala, lemon juice and sugar. Simmer, uncovered, for another 10 minutes, until the liquid has all gone.

Makes 4 to 6 servings

* if you use oil instead of butter

Cilantro Chutney

This simple-to-prepare chutney makes a wonderful accompaniment to spicy dishes.

- **1 bunch fresh cilantro, washed, finely chopped**
- **1 bunch fresh mint, finely chopped**
- **1 small onion, finely chopped**
- **1 lemon, juiced**
- **1 tsp (5 mL) sea salt**

Blend the cilantro, mint and onion, and then add the juice of 1 lemon and sea salt.

Makes 10 to 12 servings

Tomato Raita VG* GF

A cooling sauce that makes eating curry just perfect!

- **1 lb (454 gr) ripe tomatoes, coarsely chopped**
- **2 cups (475 mL) yogourt**
- **1 Tbsp (15 mL) chili peppers, finely minced**
- **½ bunch fresh cilantro**
- **½ tsp (2.5 mL) sea salt**
- **1 Tbsp (15 mL) vegetable oil**
- **½ tsp (2.5 mL) dried red peppers, crushed**
- **1½ tsp (7.5 mL) mustard seeds, roasted**

Put the tomatoes in a good-sized bowl and add the yogourt, chilies, cilantro and salt. Stir.

Heat the oil on a cast-iron griddle or in a frying pan, and add the crushed peppers and mustard seeds, shaking until the seeds are crackling.

Stir quickly into the yogourt mixture and chill a few hours before serving.

Makes 8 servings

* if you use soy yogourt

No Peeping Basmati Rice VG GF

If you want perfect rice, just remember there can be no peeping!

4 cups (1 L) cold water

2 cups (475 mL) basmati rice, thoroughly washed under running water

1 bay leaf

Add the well-rinsed rice to the cold water and toss in the bay leaf. Bring to the boil uncovered. Reduce the heat to low, put a tight-fitting lid on the saucepan and simmer (15 minutes for white basmati, 30 minutes for brown).

TIP: Never lift the lid while the rice is cooking, as this allows steam to escape. At the end of the allotted time, remove the saucepan from the heat. Inside, you will have perfectly cooked fluffy rice.

Makes 8 servings

Garam Masala   VG GF

Add this fragrant blend of spices to curried dishes.

2 Tbsp (30 mL) cardamom pods

2 Tbsp (30 mL) peppercorns

2 Tbsp (30 mL) cumin seeds

2 (1 oz/28 gr) cinnamon sticks, broken into 2-inch (5-cm) pieces

2 tsp (10 mL) whole cloves

½ tsp (2.5 mL) fresh-grated nutmeg

4 Tbsp (60 mL) coriander seeds

Spread all the spices onto a baking sheet and roast in a low 200F (95C) oven for 25 minutes, stirring occasionally to prevent scorching.

Remove from the oven and grind all the spices in a food processor or coffee grinder until well powdered.

Store in an airtight spice jar in a cool, dark cupboard.

Makes about 1½ cups (350 mL)

Baked Apple Dessert

This dessert is positively yummy served warm or cold, with or without Greek yogourt, ice cream or whipped cream.

4 large cooking apples, peeled, cored, cut into ½-inch (1-cm) slices (see Apple Peeler, page 32)

½ cup (125 mL) water

Filling

½ cup (125 mL) dried fruit—currants, raisins, cherries

1 Tbsp (15 mL) hazelnuts, almonds or walnuts, chopped

¼ cup (60 mL) raw cane sugar

1 tsp (5 mL) cinnamon powder

2 Tbsp (30 mL) butter, cut into chunks

Preheat oven to 375F (190C).

Put the slices back together again to make the whole apple, and stand it upright in a buttered 8-inch (20-cm) square baking dish.

Blend the filling ingredients together into a smooth paste, and stuff the paste into the core of each apple from top to bottom.

Pour ½ cup (125 mL) water into the dish.

Reduce oven heat to 350F (175C) and bake for 30 minutes until the apples are soft.

Makes 4 servings

Below: Baked apples topped with homemade yogourt.

Scrummy Applesauce `VG` `GF`

In the fall, you can turn apples into applesauce in no time by using a food mill (see page 32), which not only makes the job faster, but also means a better sauce. Puréeing the cooked sauce through the mill removes peels and cores, and leaves all the goodness of the apples in the dish.

12 large apples, quartered
Water
Juice of 1 lemon

Place enough water to fill a large saucepan 1 inch (2.5 cm) deep and add the juice of 1 lemon, which stops the apples from browning. As you chop the apples, throw them into the saucepan, stirring to coat with lemon water.

Gradually bring to the boil, stirring to prevent sticking, and then reduce the heat to medium. When the saucepan is full, turn the heat down to low, and slowly cook the apples for 25 to 30 minutes, stirring occasionally to prevent sticking, until the sauce is soft and smooth.

Purée the sauce through a food mill.

Applesauce keeps well refrigerated. It can also be frozen in tubs or processed in quart Mason jars for 25 minutes in a boiling-water canner for longer storage (see Home Canning, page 77).

Optional additions
Sweeten with ½ cup (125 mL) maple syrup or raw cane sugar.
Spice with ground cinnamon and/or grated nutmeg.
Add ½ cup (125 mL) dried fruit—currants, raisins or cherries—presoaked in hot water.

Makes 2 cups (475 mL)

Spiced Applesauce Cake

This is one of my favourite coffee cakes, because it's so moist and aromatic. Freeze some between layers of waxed paper for unexpected guests, because it won't last long when you put it in the cake tin!

- ¼ cup (60 mL) butter, at room temperature
- 1 cup (250 mL) brown sugar
- 1 egg, beaten
- 1 cup (250 mL) unbleached white flour
- ¾ cups (180 mL) whole wheat flour
- 1 tsp (5 mL) baking soda
- 1 tsp (5 mL) ground cinnamon
- ½ tsp (2.5 mL) grated whole nutmeg
- ½ tsp (2.5 mL) ground cloves
- ½ tsp (2.5 mL) ground cardamom seeds
- 1 cup (250 mL) warm applesauce (see Scrummy Applesauce, page 243)
- 1 cup (250 mL) raisins or dried goji berries
- 1 cup (250 mL) walnut, chopped, plus (optionally) 2 Tbsp (30 mL) extra for garnish
- 1 batch Cream-Cheese Frosting (page 143)

Preheat oven to 350F (175C).

Beat the butter and the sugar until light and fluffy. Using a wooden spoon, gradually add the beaten egg to form a smooth batter.

Sift the flour(s) with the baking soda and the spices and gradually add to the batter, blending in well with a wooden spoon.

Add the applesauce, dried fruit and nuts and blend well.

Use a spatula to scoop out the batter and smooth into a greased 8-inch (20-cm) square baking pan.

Bake for 35 to 40 minutes, until firm to the touch in the centre, when a toothpick comes out clean. Leave to cool on a baking rack.

Spread frosting over the top and sides of the cooled cake.

If desired, garnish with finely chopped nuts.

Makes sixteen 2-inch (5-cm) squares of cake

Sugar Plums   VG GF

These are wonderful sweet and spicy treats for the Christmas season. For some family fun, get the kids involved in making them! And plan a day ahead to soak the nuts to make them healthy as can be (see page 41).

- **1 cup (250 mL) walnuts or hazelnuts**
- **½ tsp (2.5 mL) sea salt**
- **1 orange, peel and zest**
- **1 tsp (5 mL) ground cinnamon**
- **½ tsp (2.5 mL) fresh-grated nutmeg**
- **¼ tsp (1 mL) ground allspice**
- **¼ tsp (1 mL) ground ginger**
- **¼ tsp (1 mL) ground coriander**
- **1 cup (250 mL) dried cherries, strawberries or blueberries**
- **1 cup (250 mL) dried apricots, figs or prunes, chopped**
- **1 cup (250 mL) unsweetened desiccated coconut**

Toss the nuts in a bowl with the salt and just cover with warm water. Allow to soak in the lightly salted water for 8 hours or overnight.* Drain and rinse well.

Put the presoaked nuts into a food processor bowl with the orange peel and zest, spices and all the dried fruit except for the coconut. Pulse the mixture a few times to combine, and then process as needed to form a paste.

Shape the sugar plums by forming 2 Tbsp (30 mL) of paste into a ball, and rolling it in the coconut.

Makes 36 sugar plums

* Soaking nuts improves flavour by releasing bitter tannins into the water. It also improves digestion by neutralizing enzyme inhibitors naturally present in nuts. See Why You Should Soak Nuts, page 41 for more details.

Natural Fruitcake

This is my wholesome alternative to commercial fruitcakes that contain preservatives, artificial flavours and colours. This cake is best made six weeks before Christmas, because it improves with age. Store in a cool, dark place. Plan to make it a day ahead because it benefits from an overnight soaking of the dried fruit. Make it even merrier by wrapping it in cheesecloth soaked in rum or sherry, and enhance the flavour by presoaking the fruit overnight in sherry or orange juice before baking.

Fruit Mixture

  1 lb (454 gr) dark raisins

  1 lb (454 gr) golden raisins

  1 lb (454 gr) dried currants

  4 oz (112 gr) dried cranberries

  4 oz (112 gr) dried cherries

  8 oz (225 gr) dried apricots, chopped

  8 oz (225 gr) almonds, toasted and finely chopped

  1 lemon, grated peel

  1 orange, grated peel

  1 cup (250 mL) sherry or orange juice (optional)

Cake

  1 cup (250 mL) butter, softened

  ½ cup (125 mL) liquid honey

  ½ cup (125 mL) molasses

  2 tsp (10 mL) pure vanilla extract

  2 tsp (10 mL) pure almond extract

  ½ lemon, juiced

  6 eggs, at room temperature, beaten

  2¾ cups (655 mL) whole wheat flour

  1 tsp (5 mL) baking soda

  1 tsp (5 mL) each of mace, cinnamon, allspice, nutmeg

  ½ tsp (2.5 mL) ground ginger

  ½ tsp (2.5 mL) sea salt

  ¼ tsp (1 mL) ground cloves

Plump up the fruit and enhance its flavour by soaking it overnight in 1 cup (250 mL) sherry or 1 cup (250 mL) orange juice if alcohol is not your thing. Drain before using.

Preheat oven to 275F (135C).

In a large bowl, blend the butter, honey, molasses, vanilla and almond extract and juice of half a lemon together. In a separate bowl, beat the eggs until thick and lemon-coloured and then slowly add to the batter until smooth.

Mix all the dry ingredients together well.

Add 1½ cups (350 mL) of dry mixture to the batter and blend well. Then gradually blend in the rest of the dry ingredients.

Add the fruit mixture to the batter and blend everything together thoroughly.

Prepare the cake pans (large, medium or small) by lining them with greased parchment paper. Fill the cake pans three quarters full with the cake mixture.

TIPS: Tie a double band of brown paper around the outside of the cake pan(s) to prevent the sides of the cake from becoming burnt during baking. Place a baking pan filled with hot water in the oven during baking to stop the cake(s) from drying out.

Bake at 275F (135C).

1 large cake: 3½ to 4 hours

2 medium cakes: 2¾ to 3 hours

3 small cakes: 2 hours

Winter Drinks

Mulled Spice Wine   VG* GF

Offering this seasonal drink to house guests on a cold winter's night not only warms them up, but puts them in the mood for the festivities to follow.

- 1 cup (250 mL) apple juice
- 3¼ cups (760 mL) organic red wine, full bodied (e.g., Cabernet Sauvignon or Shiraz)
- 4 Tbsp (60 mL) liquid honey
- 3 cinnamon sticks, chopped up
- 3 whole star anise
- 3 whole cloves
- 2 whole peppercorns
- 2 cardamom pods
- **Optional: Brandy to taste**

Wrap the spices in a cheesecloth bag, twist and tie with a piece of cotton string. Add the spice bag to the apple juice, wine and honey and gradually heat over low-medium heat, but do not allow to boil.

Keep at a gentle simmer for 20 minutes.

Remove the bag of spices. Stir in the brandy if using and ladle into heat-tolerant punch cups.

Makes 4 to 6 servings

* if you use maple syrup instead of honey

INDEX